SUMMONS TO SERVE

SUMMONS TO SERVE
The Christian call to prison ministry

Richard Atherton

Geoffrey Chapman
London

A Geoffrey Chapman book published by
Cassell Publishers Limited
Artillery House, Artillery Row, London SW1P 1RT

First published in 1987

ISBN 0 225 66497 6

British Library Cataloguing in Publication Data
Atherton, Richard
  Summons to serve: the Christian call to prison ministry.
  1. Chaplains, Prison—Great Britain
  I. Title
  365'.66   HV8867

Printed and bound in Great Britain by
Biddles Ltd, Guildford and King's Lynn

CONTENTS

This book is dedicated to all my brothers and sisters 'inside' and especially to those who appear, albeit under pseudonyms, in the pages that follow.

I also acknowledge my gratitude to Sister Madeleine Sheridan, DC, for the skill and endless patience she showed in the typing of the manuscript; and to Simon Atherton who drew the maps in Appendix B.

FOREWORD

I am glad to welcome this book as an effective attempt to bridge the gap between the world of prison and the world outside. It is remarkable in that it reveals the professional experience of the prison chaplain and the compassionate but practical understanding of the priest concerned with the spiritual, emotional and human needs of those in his care. To break down the barriers which are far more profound than prison walls, the chaplain must regard his charge as would any parish priest seeking to serve his parishioners. The barriers of fear or unconcern must come down if those who have lost their freedom are to be helped to recognise Christ in their circumstances of constraint.

Behind that word 'constraint' is the loss of freedom and in practice much more besides: a close relationship with loved ones; privacy (which is not the same as 'solitary'); freedom of dress, of the clock, of the ability to take exercise. In one sense only the freedom of belief and thought can remain, and at times that can be threatened. If belief becomes almost the only untouchable possession, it is not surprising that ecumenism is difficult; sharing in religious loyalties can be invasion of the most sacred. Yet this book shows the opportunity for joint endeavours amidst the need for special understanding.

This book is not short of reminiscence or experience. Nor is it an attempt to regard prison or prisoners through rose-tinted spectacles. It embodies respect for the individual and above all it is an attempt to shed the light of the gospel on the lives and circumstances of an enforced community with bonds and relationships which are real. Yet it is evident that the prison chaplain cannot act alone. His ministry, like that of all pastors, requires the collaboration and support of those around him. The hope is that this book will help to bring about the supportive and prayerful interest of many who have never seen beyond a prison wall from the outside: and at the same time perhaps be some encouragement to those whose work or temporary confinement lies within.

To be concerned with prison life, even as a prisoner, is not all deprivation. At one time I visited regularly a prison where all the inmates were 'lifers' and I saw how with patient help they grew in mutual responsibility and in some cases religious faith. Now, many years later, I still hear from some of them at Christmas and Easter, in recollection of special times and special celebrations in the past. One Christmas, one of them who had just obtained his release wrote to assure me that as he 'walked along the pavement' to midnight Mass he would remember those with whom he had shared Christmas in the past. That phrase 'as I walk along the pavement' perhaps reveals something of what is lost 'inside'. Its rediscovery owes much to Monsignor Atherton and his colleagues.

25th March 1987

† Derek Worlock
Archbishop of Liverpool

1

LOOK BACK WITH GRATITUDE

The desert will rejoice, and flowers will bloom in the wilderness. The desert will sing and shout for joy.

(Isaiah 35:1–2: *Good News Bible*)

Jesus Christ once told his friends: 'You will be my witnesses not only in Jerusalem but throughout Judea and Samaria, and indeed to the ends of the earth' (Acts 1:8). There is undoubtedly a sense in which prison chaplains and all who share in the prison ministry may be numbered among those who witness 'to the ends of the earth'. Indeed, in times gone by, criminals were transported literally to the other side of the world, as far away as possible from decent, law-abiding citizens. Nowadays, in a different yet hardly less effective way, they are transported to another world, a strange world so different from what they have known, and far removed from the sight and the thoughts of most other people. And so, though the modern prison chaplain may find himself in an establishment sited in the heart of a great city, its massive walls and iron bars and clanging gates, and even the bunch of keys that dangle heavily at his own waist, serve as a constant reminder that his parishioners are the outcasts of society. He knows, of course, they they have been found guilty of crime, perhaps crime of the most sickening kind; that some of them – though very few in fact – are apparently professional criminals, hard and unrepentant and committed to evil ways; that many of them are extremely selfish; that most are weak and unreliable. But he knows other things too about the men and women the Lord has given him.

He quickly learns that by and large they are the poorer, the less privileged, the more handicapped members of the community. He realises that 'criminal' and 'sinner' are not necessarily interchangeable terms, for 'the Lord does not see as man sees; men judge by appearances but the Lord judges by the heart' (1 Sam 16:7). Indeed, some of the offences most bitterly condemned by the Master – pride, for example, or hypocrisy, or uncharity – may be committed with impunity so far as the courts of the land are concerned. He sometimes wonders if the majority of his people should not be regarded as the 'damaged goods' of society. Certainly a great number of them might have come straight from the pages of the Gospel – the lonely, the unloved, the addicted, the inadequate, the emotionally disturbed. He is not surprised to find that when he enters the prison world his Master is already there: 'I was in prison and you visited me' (Matt 25).

A prison Medical Officer once described the prison chaplain as a bridge-builder, someone who ensures that each 'island' is connected with the 'mainland'. That is perhaps not a bad way of putting it. Of all the members of the prison staff – governors and assistant governors, medical officers and psychologists, welfare officers and prison officers – the priest is the one figure already familiar to every member of his inmate flock, even to those who have never been 'inside' before. They remember that he (or at any rate a colleague like him) used to visit them in school when they were children, called to see them in their homes, perhaps prepared them for marriage, buried their dead, baptised their children. And so they know that he is present now not because they are sick, not because they have to be processed into a new community, not because they are in need of case-work, not even (or at least not primarily) because they are criminals, but quite simply because they are men and women. A young prisoner summed it up perfectly. When he was asked why a priest should work in prison, he replied: 'Because we're people, just like the people outside'.

The prison chaplain, then, is an obvious link between them and the mainland of the world outside and, more importantly, between them and the great family circle of the Church. His very presence bears witness to the fact that no matter how terrible a mess they may have made of their lives, no matter how they have been rejected by society at large, the Church, and indeed Christ himself, still cares for them, still accepts them, is still anxious to help them.

Looking back over my own years spent in prison, I am confronted with a kaleidoscope of memories: the endless series of interviews with 'receptions', new arrivals who need to be assured that I come to them as a friend, a brother in Christ; sharing confidences and offering counsel; clambering onto the prison roof in an attempt (unsuccessful, as it turned out) to talk down one of my 'sheep' that had gone astray; visiting those who are sick in the prison hospital and those who are in solitary confinement because of their infringement of prison discipline; writing innumerable letters, making 'phone calls, completing reports, visiting families, striving to reconcile estranged husbands and wives; sitting in a dingy cell, breaking the sad news of a bereavement and then providing the comfort and support desperately needed by a man who feels so helpless and so hopeless in his grief; sometimes being surprised, and even put to shame, by the faith and simple charity of my friends 'inside': I can understand the chaplain who said to me: 'I often wonder if I'm not the one who stands in greater need of conversion than many of the fellows in here'; burying old Joe who at death was without a friend in the world except myself; assisting in a prison chapel at one of the first Masses of a newly ordained priest whose father, serving a sentence for an offence more technical than criminal, was the only other member of the congregation; trying to enter into the elations and the heartbreaks, the laughter and the despair of those committed to my care; working alongside other members of staff and striving to make my own contribution to their deliberations, my contribution as a Christian and as a priest. And of course, the culminating point where all my other activities meet: the celebration of the sacraments and the preaching of the word.

Using the imagery of Scripture, I like to think of prison as a desert; a place where the human spirit may be purified and ennobled but, alas, more easily twisted and damaged; a place that is often threatening and almost always unpredictable; a place where faith is put to the test – the faith of the inmates, but that of their pastor too; a place of loneliness and powerlessness and frustration, where a man (and especially a priest) begins to feel in his bones the truth of our Lord's words: 'Without me you can do nothing' (John 15:5); and so ultimately a place of encounter with God.

Especially in this desert place a priest comes to see that he has no worthwhile witness to bear, no matter how many and how varied his activities, unless he can bring to his prisoners the heart of the Christian message, which is Jesus Christ himself. One of our most dedicated chaplains, who initially had found prison life so alien, eventually wrote to me saying: 'When I arrived here four years ago, my first impression was that it was a God-forsaken hole. Yet soon I was to discover the power and the love and the beauty of God shining through all the suffering'. His letter put me in mind of that passage in the book of Exodus which describes how the people of Israel, having at last accomplished their trek through the desert, 'looked steadfastly towards the wilderness', back towards the desert through which they had come, and there, in that most improbable place, 'they saw the glory of the Lord' (Ex 16:10).

It is many years ago since the day when the huge wooden outer door closed behind me and, through the open metalwork of the gate ahead, I caught my first glimpse at close quarters of Her Majesty's Prison, Liverpool, with its bleak façade broken only by rows of small barred windows.

By a strange oversight it was not until long after the event that I realised that the day of my arrival as chaplain, 1 December, had also been the anniversary date of the death of Brother Charles de Foucauld, a date dear to his followers and admirers. A strange oversight because in ministering to my friends 'inside' I have always drawn immense inspiration from the life of Brother Charles, the man from the desert, the man who, like many a prisoner, had once been written off as a hopeless failure but proved his critics to be woefully wrong. Charles de Foucauld was a man whose heart was big with love for God and men; who found his inspiration in the pages of the Gospel and in long hours of Eucharistic prayer, where he was filled with the desire to become like his 'beloved Brother and Lord'; who saw his vocation to be 'among the sickest souls, the most abandoned sheep ... those to whom Jesus would go'; who wanted all men to look upon him as a brother, who wanted 'to shout the Gospel through my whole life'; who longed to be 'patient as God is patient, loving as God is loving'; who was ready to give himself to the point of exhaustion to all who came his way. Set against this daunting ideal, a prison chaplain feels that he has scarcely even begun to fulfil the commission that has been entrusted to him.

I realise that, like St Paul, I can boast that 'I have been in prisons often' (2 Cor 11:23), and yet I know that my boasting is of no avail except in the measure that, like him, I have been able to say: 'Be imitators of me as I am of Christ' (1 Cor 11:1). For the witness of the prison priest is not complete when he acts as bridge-builder to the mainland of the world outside, or even to the Church at large, but only when by his speaking, his doing and, above all, by his living, he is a 'revelation' to his flock of Jesus Christ, for he is our only Way to the Father, the only bridge-builder that can connect every island (whether clad in prison bluey-grey or clerical black) with the mainland and the homeland of heaven.

A fortnight ago I received a letter from a man who has devoted virtually all his adult life to work with and for prisoners and ex-prisoners, both in the community and 'inside'. He referred, with a certain sadness, to 'this important and yet most misunderstood apostolate'. This book is an attempt to remove some of the misunderstandings which surround a ministry of its nature lying hidden away at 'the ends of the earth'.

Thus, its three central chapters – 4, 5 and 6 – aim to reveal, so far as it is possible in words, what life is like in a big local prison ('Prison Parish'), to encourage a more informed and therefore more sensitive attitude towards prisoners and prison staff ('Prison Parishioners'), and to provide an account of the mission of the prison chaplain ('Prison Pastor'). These central chapters are preceded by two others (2 and 3) which deal with the motivation for the chaplain's ministry ('Rooted in the Gospels') and the historical setting of that ministry ('Penal History and the Prison Chaplain'); and it is followed by another two (7 and 8) which are concerned with issues which every chaplain has to face up to in some measure: the origins of criminal behaviour ('Focusing on Crime') and the justifications usually given for punishing wrongdoers ('Punish and be Damned?').

Chapter 9 ('The Church and the Prisoner') insists that though chaplains may be in the forefront of prison ministry, the responsibility for that ministry rests with the whole Christian Church and is a constant challenge to all Christians. The final chapter ('Lessons I Have Learned "Inside"'), like this first, is in some sense a personal testimony as I look back in gratitude on the years I have been privileged to share in an apostolate which has given me the opportunity to 'visit' Jesus in prison and which has been such a formative experience for me, as a human being and as a Christian.

Much of what I have written reflects, I believe, what is held by most of my chaplain colleagues, but the final responsibility for all views expressed is entirely mine. In the course of writing I have often recalled a prayer, first brought to my attention by a veteran prison visitor. It is a prayer I make my own:

Dear Lord, be merciful to those who must pay for their sins.
And, Lord, please keep mine a secret. Amen.

2

ROOTED IN THE GOSPELS

I do not think there is a Gospel phrase which has made a deeper impression on me and transformed my life more than this one: 'Insofar as you did this to one of the least of these brothers of mine, you did it to me'. One has only to think that these words were spoken by the uncreated Truth, who also said, 'This is my body ... This is my blood ... '.

(Brother Charles de Foucauld)[1]

It was a perfect spring morning, the ideal occasion, it seemed, for keeping the great feast of Easter. The prisoners who had attended chapel were back in their cells, some of them visibly happier after proclaiming in worship with Christians everywhere that: 'Jesus is Risen'. The service had been led by the bishop, and as I accompanied him along the flagged corridors of the prison wings towards his car, I thanked him for joining us and sharing in our Eucharist. He stopped in his tracks and turned towards me. 'You mustn't thank me', he said. 'Visiting the imprisoned – that's the sort of thing which makes a bishop's life worthwhile.'

He spoke with such evident sincerity that his words stayed with me, and many years later their significance was brought into sharper focus during a visit that another chaplain and I paid to Cardinal Hume. Towards the end of the meeting he told me that, in a sense, he envied us the work we were doing. 'You could hardly be involved', he explained, 'in a ministry more deeply rooted in the Gospels.'

This chapter is an attempt, first to uncover the *gospel foundation* of the prison apostolate, and, second, to give some indication of how those foundations have been built upon by *the witness of Christian people*.

Gospel foundations for prison ministry

Mark: This is the briefest and, according to the commonly accepted view of experts, the most ancient of the four gospels. Like the others, it does not attempt to recount all that Jesus said and did: it is simply one approach to his life and ministry, an approach determined to a large extent by the needs of the Christian community for which Mark wrote, some thirty years after the death and resurrection of our Lord.

It is more concerned with actions than with words, but the actions of Jesus have an eloquence of their own. And so it is more than coincidental that the first glimpse we catch of him in Mark's gospel is one in which he takes his place among the crowd of people, along the banks of the river Jordan, who are waiting to confess their sins and to be baptised by John. Jesus is the sinless one and yet he begins his career by identifying himself with sinners. The standard has been set. In the following chapters he is involved in a score of miracles, almost all of them affecting people who were normally treated as outcasts, sinners, rejects of society. He touches untouchables, like the leper (1:40–45), and allows himself, or at any rate his garments, to be touched by a woman who would be regarded as unclean (5:28). When he comes to choose his special friends, the fifth on the list is a tax-collector (2:13–14), and in the Palestine of the first century tax-collectors, who worked for the Roman powers of occupation and often enough indulged in crooked practices, were looked upon as very unsavoury characters. Not only does Jesus pick one of these men as his disciple, but he goes and has a meal with him in his house, where he is surrounded by 'tax-collectors and sinners'. And when others protest at his keeping such disreputable company, he proclaims: 'It is not the healthy who need the doctor, but the sick. I did not come to call the virtuous, but sinners' (2:17). Reflecting on this verse, Charles de Foucauld wrote: 'There should be only one desire in my heart, to give Jesus to all men. I should be especially concerned for the lost sheep, the sinners, not leaving the ninety-nine lost sheep in order to stay quietly in the field with the faithful one'.[2]

It has often been noted that though Mark tends to move along at almost breathless speed, giving no more than a brisk account of various events, he unexpectedly adopts a much more leisurely pace when he comes to tell the story of the martyrdom of John the Baptist. (His account is longer than that of any other gospel writer.) And the explanation would seem to be that Mark wants us to understand that since John is the precursor, the forerunner of Jesus, what happened to him – arrest, imprisonment, execution – will happen to Jesus also. In fact, it is the story of Jesus' Passion which attracts Mark most powerfully; not only does it take up a disproportionate part of his gospel – almost a quarter of the whole – but it is also being prepared for, pointed to, hinted at, time and time again. So much so that the gospel has sometimes been described as 'a Passion narrative with a lengthy introduction'.[3]

If there is much in the earlier part of Mark's gospel which offers support and encouragement to those who work with and for prisoners, there is even more in its final chapters. There the Jesus who at the outset of the ministry identified himself with outcasts, now actually becomes one of them. He is himself a prisoner, he shares the company and the fate of prisoners. 'His own' had all 'deserted him and fled' (14:50) when the testing came, and ironically it is the officer, in charge of the execution squad, who is able to recognise in the dead Jesus flanked by condemned criminals the 'Son of God' (15:39).

In one prison I was fascinated to come across a large picture of the Last Supper, painted by a prisoner, in which all the Apostles and our Lord himself are wearing prison uniform. There was no doubt in the mind of that prisoner-artist that the Jesus of the gospels has made himself completely one with the imprisoned everywhere.

Matthew: This gospel, long and carefully structured, may not have instant appeal for the modern Christian, though in times gone by it was the most popular of all. In particular, its style may appear laborious and even a little dreary when compared with the rugged, racy style of Mark. However, it is no less insistent that Jesus' 'preferential option' is for the poor, the hurt, the vulnerable; and, as we shall see, it provides the key-text for ministry among the imprisoned: 'You visited *ME*'.

A striking feature of Matthew's gospel, presumably because its first readers were mostly convert Jews, is its constant attempts to show how in Jesus the prophecies of the Old Testament have reached their fulfilment. One of the loveliest of those prophecies, recounted by Matthew in 12:18–21, depicts the long-awaited Messiah in terms that have a special relevance for those engaged in the prison apostolate: as a Servant, gentle, spirit-filled, non-judgemental, compassionate. In fact part of the prophecy, 'He will not break the crushed reed, nor put out the smouldering wick', has provided the motto and the inspiration for the badge of Prison Fellowship, an interdenominational organisation working for prisoners in many parts of the world.

It is in Matthew's gospel, also, that Jesus is presented as a teacher, a new and greater Moses. The best known and loved of all his teachings was delivered on a mountain top, just as Moses had brought down from the heights of Mount Sinai the laws of God and taught them with authority. The Sermon on the Mount (5 – 7), with its repetition of: 'You have heard that it was said of old ... but I say to you ... ', sets the new and loftier standards that are to prevail among Jesus' followers. There is talk of being reconciled at all costs with our brother who has wronged us (5:23–26), of turning the other cheek (5:39), of loving enemies and praying for those who persecute us (5:44), of forgiving as we ourselves ask for forgiveness (6:12), of not judging, if we wish to escape judgement (7:1), of not drawing attention to the splinter in our brother's eye while unaware of the plank in our own (7:3), of treating others as we would like them to treat us (7:12). However these sayings are to be understood when organising social institutions – few people, I imagine, would follow Tolstoy in interpreting them as a command to get rid of law-courts – they surely lay upon individual Christians the obligation of adopting a peculiarly Christ-like attitude towards wrongdoers of every kind.

As a prison chaplain, I have found deep significance in the little parable, peculiar to the gospel of Matthew, of the two sons (21:28–32) who were asked by their father to do some work for him. One said: 'Certainly, of course I will', but in fact did nothing. The other began by refusing but then had second thoughts and responded to his father's request. It is a story which warns us against facile judgements and encourages us to recognise that things are not always what they seem to be. And that is a sound piece of advice for anyone who is tramping along the landings of a prison – or, for that matter, sitting in the awesome surroundings of the Crown court. It is Jesus himself who makes the point of the tale when he tells the religious leaders to their faces: 'I tell you solemnly, tax-collectors and prostitutes are making their way into the kingdom before you' (21:31).

And so we move on to what might be described as the Magna Carta of the prison ministry, that drama of the Last Judgement, portrayed so magnificently in chapter 25, where 'the Son of Man' takes 'his seat on his throne of glory' and begins to 'separate men from one another as the shepherd separates sheep from goats'. The 'sheep' are invited to inherit the eternal kingdom because (among other things) 'I was ... in prison, and you came to see me', while the 'goats' are debarred from the kingdom because 'I was ... in prison, and you never visited me'. Indeed, the King solemnly explains, whatever you did or failed to do 'to one of the least of these brothers of mine, you did or neglected to do it to me'.

In his book *Resurrection*, the distinguished Anglican theologian Rowan Williams comments movingly yet realistically on this passage in which Jesus identified himself with *all* powerless victims whether they be innocent or (to our scandal) guilty. 'How difficult it is for us', he admits, 'to see the face of God as victim in a criminal in prison?' This, he point out, is not of course to suggest that God is indifferent to wrongdoing, nor that we are at fault in experiencing anger against the evil done or taking action against its perpetrator. But it does mean, he continues, 'that the hopelessness and self-loathing, even the impotent anger of the jailed murderer, all that constitutes him or her a trapped and helpless victim, must speak to us, in however distorted an accent, of the Lamb of God. Our necessary justice does not repair the breach, which we are all too willing to see as unbridgeable, as final. But if God is the enemy of all human diminution, he is there too: he is there as the "Unfinished-ness" of our relation to the criminal, as the muted question, the half-heard cry for some unimaginable qualitative leap into reconcilia-tion. He is there guaranteeing that we shall not forget even the most loathed and despised of victims'.[4]

In a sermon to prison chaplains, the German theologian Karl Rahner returns to the same passage in the gospel of Matthew and shows its peculiar relevance to them and their ministry: 'I think that the first thing for you to do is simply to rejoice over these words. They apply to you without any kind of translation, just as they were spoken then ... There are few vocations with such words to rejoice over, few that find themselves being addressed in so unchanged a fashion by the mouth of the Son of Man ... When the last day comes, we shall still be amongst those who ask wonderingly, just as much as those who have not visited the Lord and not found him, "When did we see thee in prison, and visit thee?" (Mt 25:39, 44). As far as *experience* goes it will always be like this. It will seem to us that it is not he, that it is not possible to find him in the prisoners. But this is precisely what Christianity is, this finding when we think we have not found, this seeing when we seem to be gazing into darkness, this having when we think that we have lost. And so it is here.'[5]

Perhaps it is not too surprising that this Church-orientated gospel (in fact the only one containing explicit references to the Church, cf. 16:18 and 18:17), which begins with the affirmation that Jesus is 'Emmanuel – God-with-us' (1:23) and ends with the promise that he will be 'with you always; yes, to the end of time' (28:20), should describe the fate of Jesus' followers (the Church) in terms of whether or not they have allowed him to continue his mission among the hungry and the thirsty, the strangers and the naked, the sick – and the imprisoned.

Luke: This gospel is really part I of a two-volume work, part II being the Acts of the Apostles. Both are characterised by a sense of movement and direction, a missionary spirit; Jesus makes the momentous journey from Galilee to Jerusalem, the heart of Judaism (cf. Lk 4:9–19); the apostles take the good news from Jerusalem 'to the ends of the earth' (Acts).

It is Luke who traces Jesus' ancestry back not to Abraham, the Father of the Jewish race (cf. Matt 1), but to Adam, the Father of the human race (3:23–38). This is the universal gospel. It presents our Lord as saviour of all mankind, Jew and Gentile alike, but it also insists that he is especially Saviour of the men and women who are on the periphery of society, the 'marginalised', as we might call them today. It is supremely the gospel of the compassion of Christ. As W. D. Davies wrote: 'The Jesus of Luke, one feels, might well have uttered the words written on the Statue of Liberty in New York harbour: "Give me your tired, your poor, your huddled masses yearning to breathe free. Send these, the homeless, tempest-tost to me"'.[6] Deep concern for the least and for the lost, already apparent in the gospel of Mark and a characteristic attitude of church life in the gospel of Matthew, dominates the gospel of Luke.

To get the 'feel' of this gospel it would be hard to find a better point of entry than in the event described in chapter 4, verses 16 to 22. Our Lord has returned to his native town of Nazareth and is attending a service in the local synagogue. When invited to preach he carefully chooses these words of Isaiah:

The spirit of the Lord has been given to me,
for he has anointed me.
He has sent me to bring good news to the poor,

to proclaim liberty to captives
and to the blind new sight,
to set the downtrodden free,
to proclaim the Lord's year of favour.

The words were full of Messianic import, as his listeners well knew. No wonder 'all eyes in the synagogue were fixed on him' (4:20).

The reading over, he sat down to preach, as a rabbi would. And then – the bombshell. 'This text', he announced, 'is being fulfilled today even as you listen' (4:21–22). 'Yesterday', the day of prophecy, the day of promise and of waiting, is over. The 'today' of fulfilment has arrived; the 'today' of the Messiah has come. And he takes the words of Isaiah as the text for his inuagural address. It is a summary of Jesus' programme, but also a summary of the gospel itself. In the pages of Luke we see that programme being implemented – 'good news for the poor', 'release for prisoners', 'new sight for the blind', 'freedom for the oppressed'. It seems to me that the more closely we examine the Isaiah text the more we come to realise that it is a fairly accurate description of the prison chaplain's programme also: he too is in business to preach the good news, to bring freedom to captives, to offer new vision to the blind.

In one of his lectures, the American Scripture scholar Barnabas Ahearne, CP, compared Luke's gospel to a rogues' gallery. Certainly, in Luke we come across a procession of unlikely characters that are to be found in no other gospel. Some appear in real-life events, like the girl who was a sinner but won the approval of Jesus (7:36–50); many more in parables, like the good Samaritan (10:29–37), or the prodigal son (15:11–32), or the tax-collector in the Temple who simply beat his breast and said 'God be merciful to me a sinner' (18:9–14). (There is even one parable (12:39–40) in which our Lord compares himself to a burglar. Let no one say that Jesus lacked a sense of humour!) The story of Zacchaeus (19:1–10) is a typical example: the diminutive tax-gatherer was at the top of the tree – in more ways than one – when Jesus brought him down to earth, accompanied him to his home and softened his greedy, grasping heart to the point of conversion; and then announced: 'Today' (the Messianic 'today') 'salvation has come to this house, for the Son of Man has come to seek out and save what was lost'.

It is Luke who highlights Jesus' role as 'the friend of sinners', and step by step it prepares us for the culminating scene on Calvary, where Jesus, apparently friendless in his final anguish, is befriended by a prisoner, a condemned criminal (23:39–43). 'Jesus, remember me when you come into your kingdom', the criminal cries, and in response the thorn-crowned head turns towards him and speaks words which no other creature has ever heard from the lips of Jesus: 'Today you will be with me in paradise'. The 'Today' announced in the synagogue at Nazareth has now reached its climax and its first beneficiary is a wrongdoer. On Good Friday afternoon Jesus returns to 'his Father's house', with a repentant thief at his side.

Some years ago a prisoner who had spent a good deal of his young life 'inside' was transferred to a new prison. He had left us in a letter an account of what happened next. 'I was placed in a cell where I discovered a Bible which had been left there by my predecessor, and I felt an irresistible urge to flip through the pages of the old book. To me that's what the Bible was, an old book, nothing more. Little by little as I read it I came to realise that it wasn't an ordinary old book, it was as though each verse were addressed to me personally. I learned from this book that a certain Jesus loved me and that He had loved me to the extent of dying on the cross for me. I wanted to know more about this mysterious Jesus who pardoned the girl taken in adultery and forgave the thief crucified with him. I raised my two hands which had committed so many crimes, struck so many blows, and extended them trembling and said: "Jesus, if you exist, I want you to change me, I want you because I am certainly ashamed of myself".' But the more astonishing thing came towards the end of the letter where he wrote: 'I am still in a cell as I write, but I am free, because there is greater freedom with Jesus in prison than there is outside prison without him'. This lad had discovered from personal experience the unexpected truth in our Lord's promise: he has come to set prisoners free, not only from prison but even within it.

That young man had had, though he did not put it this way, an 'Emmaus experience' (24:13–35). Many chaplains too find their 'hearts burning within them' as they make their way through the pages of this beautiful gospel.

John: The fourth gospel is different. Though it obviously tells the same story as the other three, its way of presenting the story is unique. It is more reflective. It records fewer incidents, but usually unfolds them at greater length and often in a quite dramatic way. One of those incidents of particular interest to us is the lovely story of our Lord's encounter with the woman in Samaria (chapter 4). She was doubly an outcast, first, because she was a Samaritan and, second, because she had a skeleton – in fact, five of them – in her cupboard. Yet how gently Jesus deals with her, how carefully he listens to her, how shrewdly he confronts her, how deeply he respects her. It is worth noting, also, that it is among these outcast Samaritans, these ne'er-do-wells, that Jesus finds 'fields ... already white for the harvest' (4:35).

It is John's gospel, as we have it today, that has also preserved for us the incomparable story of the young woman caught committing adultery (7:35 – 8:11). The religious leaders wanted Jesus to condemn her and even to agree to her being stoned to death; but he neatly turns the tables on them by quietly responding: 'Let him that is without sin cast the first stone' (8:7), and then he bends down, doodling with his finger in the dust, while the accusers slink away one by one. Perhaps prisons would be more salutary places – for those outside as well as those inside their walls – if the words of Jesus were inscribed above every entrance gate: 'Let him that is without sin ... '.

The Jesus of John's gospel has come not to condemn but to save (3:17, 12:47); to set people free (8:32–36); to give them fullness of life (10:10); he has come as a good shepherd (10:11–16); one who can take on his own lips the words of the prophet: 'I shall look for the lost one, bring back the stray, bandage the wounded and make the weak strong' (Ez 34:16).

John's gospel is notable for its use of symbolism: its text is often much richer in meaning than it appears at first sight. And so John refers to Jesus' miracles as 'signs': they point to something beyond themselves, they are indicators of what he has come to do. His mission is to bring good news to the poor and the sick (4:46–53; 5:1–9); new sight to the blind (9:1–38); freedom to the imprisoned (11:1–44 – it is significant that prison cells have sometimes been compared to tombs); release for the oppressed (chapter 5). The compassionate activities of Jesus, as recounted by John, are after all remarkably similar to those ascribed to him by Luke, even if they are not presented in so clear and striking a fashion.

The first half of John's gospel (chapters 1–12) centres on a series of these 'signs'–these manifestations of who Jesus really is and what he has come to do–but the final great 'sign' is the whole complex of events beginning with the Last Supper and moving on to the passion, death and resurrection (chapters 13–21), for it is these events that most clearly reveal that 'God loved the world so much as to give his only begotten Son' (3:16). It is of course at the Last Supper, as described by John, that Jesus pronounces the 'new commandment' and insists that it is by their love, for God and for each other, that his disciples will be recognised for what they are (13:34–35). If he is the vine and we, his followers, the branches (chapter 15), the vital sap of love must flow not only between him and us, but also from each of us to one another.

And what he expresses in words, he has already expressed more strikingly in deed by kneeling down at the beginning of the Supper to wash the dust-covered feet of his disciples, giving them 'an example, so that you may copy what I have done' (13:15). The true, the genuine, disciple is the one who is not afraid of getting his hands dirty, who shows his love in practical acts of service.

An Anglican priest, who served in the Prison Service Chaplaincy for over thirty years, loves to recall how one day a prisoner presented him with a large and impressive painting of the 'washing of the feet'. The chaplain looked at it for some moments and then he said: 'I think there's something missing. I want you to go away and paint in a jug of water and a dirty–a very dirty–towel'. The prisoner did as he was asked. The painting hung in the prison chapel for many years. And a prison chaplain began his round each day by drawing inspiration from the gospel of St John.

Christian witness in prisons

During the first three centuries of its existence, the Christian Church was usually a suspect, often a proscribed and sometimes a fiercely persecuted religion. Its concern with prisoners was focused almost exclusively upon bringing moral and material relief to its own members imprisoned for their faith. Early in the fourth century, however, it gained imperial approval and, with that, freedom. Within a dozen years or so the first of the great General Councils was convened at Nicaea in Asia Minor. Among the many conciliar rulings was one that urged Bishops to ensure that a group of Christian people, lay as well as clerical, would be responsible for bringing succour to the imprisoned, providing them with food and clothing, and, where possible, setting innocent people free. Throughout the succeeding sixteen-and-a-half centuries, despite failures and inadequacies arising from human sinfulness, Christians have been to the fore in showing practical concern for the imprisoned.

In Britain, some of the greatest names in penal reform were men and women who drew their inspiration from the gospels. The Quaker Elizabeth Fry (1780–1845) devoted herself especially to the women in notorious Newgate prison, where she was renowned for her Bible readings. In 1817 she began a campaign for prison reform, and in the following year gave evidence to a House of Commons Committee on the state of prisons.

Already, in the previous century, another deeply religious man, John Howard (1726–80), had produced his monumental work *The State of the Prisons* (1777), the fruit of visits to penal institutions which were eventually to take him throughout the length and breadth of Great Britain and Europe, and involve him in at least 50,000 miles of travel, most of them on horseback. He argued that every prison should have its chaplain – a man of suitable character – and its chapel, and its supply of Bibles and prayer-books: and these books should all be chained in position! Towards the end of his life he met the great John Wesley (1703–91), father of Methodism, and the two men were much impressed by each other, for Wesley, too, was one of those Christians who felt himself drawn to prison reform. Indeed, Dean Farrer, Canon of Westminster, has written of him: 'I do not think we have done sufficient honour to the work which Wesley did. He was the inaugurator of prison reform. He visited prisons and sought to improve them long before John Howard made that his special work'.[7]

However, the influence of the gospel message is to be found not only in individuals but in whole groups and organisations involved in work for prisoners and their families. Religious orders, Anglican and Roman Catholic, have made and continue to make an indispensable contribution in this field in a wide variety of ways. What may come as more of a surprise is the fact that the Probation Service, one of the key elements of the criminal justice system today owes a great deal – its very origin, some would say – to the Police Court Mission (1876–1936). That mission was a branch of the Church of England Temperance Society, whose members were the first to be invited by magistrates to supervise offenders. The Church Army is another organisation of the Church of England which is well known in penal circles. It has been coming into prisons and providing hostel accommodation for ex-prisoners since just before the turn of the century, and many of its officers have become assistant prison chaplains.

The Salvation Army, too, has been outstanding for the services it has offered to prisoners and to ex-prisoners. Finally, even this very brief account of Christian organisations engaged in prison ministry would be incomplete without reference to the Society of St Vincent de Paul which has made its own distinctive, if unobtrusive, contribution, especially by visiting the imprisoned and their families. It takes its name from the seventeenth-century saint who laboured for part of his long career among the poor and the destitute as Chaplain General to the French galleys, and did so with such outstanding zeal that he may justly be described as the doyen of prison chaplains.

On the international scene, one of the most encouraging features in the past twenty years has been the example set by successive Popes. Both by word and deed, they have demonstrated their deep concern for men and women in prison.

When on an October evening in 1958, the portly and lovable Angelo Giuseppe Roncalli – soon to be known the whole world over as 'Good Pope John' – heard the outcome of the papal election, he summed up his feelings in two Latin words taken from the book of Job: 'horrefactus sum'. He was horrified, or, to put it more colloquially, he was shattered. Yet unbelievably, only a few hours later he was suggesting to his staff that he should visit the large Regina Coeli prison on the outskirts of Rome on the very next day. Gently, it had to be pointed out that there were one or two other things that a new Pope might have to do first!

In fact, it was not until Christmas time that he managed to fulfil his plans. As he stood before his prisoner audience, he assured them that he came as 'Joseph your brother' and told them that a couple of his own cousins had been 'inside' and yet had come to no lasting harm. He had no prepared script but revealed his own deep feelings when he went on to say: 'I want my heart to be close to yours, I want to see the world through your eyes'. (Today, a plaque bearing that message is to be found in the Regina Coeli prison.) Many of his congregation, which included officers as well as prisoners, were moved to tears. A convicted murderer fell on his knees before him, begging: 'Holy Father, can there be forgiveness for the likes of me?' And received his reply as Pope John raised him to his feet and embraced him, a lovely re-enactment of the parable of the prodigal son.

Journalists may have expressed surprise that a Pope should go prison visiting, but he, as he noted in his diary, saw himself as simply fulfilling one of the corporal works of mercy, which the gospels lay upon all Christ's followers.

In 1963 John XXIII was succeeded by Giovanni Battista Montini, who as a result of his journeys abroad (then a novelty for the papacy) came to be known as 'the pilgrim Pope'. Among his less publicised pilgrimage journeys was one, in the footsteps of John XXIII, to the Regina Coeli prison in 1972. Once again the visit was much appreciated and if his predecessor had shown his down-to-earth concern by contributing towards a special Christmas dinner for all his hearers, Paul VI went one better by arranging for a small Christmas cake to be sent to every prisoner and every prison officer in Italy. (I found it easy to identify with a prisoner in this country who, having heard this story, drily commented: 'The sooner we get an English Pope the better!')

In announcing the theme for the Holy Year[8] of 1975 Pope Paul VI made explicit reference to concern for prisoners – prisoners of conscience, but also prisoners sentenced for crimes. This led directly to the inauguration in England of an annual 'Prisoners Sunday', which was later to become ecumenical in character and be extended to a 'Prisoners Week' – a week in which efforts are made to sensitise all Christians to their duties towards the imprisoned and their families.

This enterprise, still continuing after ten years and now centred exclusively on 'domestic' prisoners, is a memorial to Paul VI. But there is another, less well known, incident in the life of Giovanni Battista Montini which highlights his gospel-like attitude to prisoners. It takes us back to a much earlier period of his life and is recounted by Cardinal Nasalli Rocca, himself an inveterate prison visitor, who often comforted men due for execution when the death penalty was still in force and who once paid a visit to Wandsworth Prison, London. The story goes as follows:

'In my early days I often used to visit the women's prison in Rome. Once I had to give a day of recollection in the prison and I asked one of the Vatican Monsignori – Giovanni Battista Montini – to help me. In the morning I gave the catechetical instruction and my companion preached a meditation in the evening. Many years later a woman between 45 and 50 stopped me as I was walking through Rome. "Father", she said, "you don't know me but I remember a sermon of yours", and she explained this was in the prison. She then asked me if I had any news of the priest who was with me on that occasion; she went on to praise him and say how his words and sympathy had led her to reform her life; she had never slipped back into her old ways and was now married with a family of four. "Tell me", she said, "have they made him a parish priest?" "A bit more than that", said I, "he is now the Pope". She was absolutely taken aback and all she could say was: "If you ever see him please give him my humble thanks – he saved me".'

In his brief thirty-three days' pontificate, Paul VI's successor John Paul I scarcely had time to show his hand completely, but it is hard to believe that this informal, smiling Pope, with the unruly quiff peeping from under his white skull cap, would not have had a place in his affections for men and women in prison. In fact, several years earlier when named Patriarch of Venice, he had given an indication of his priorities by paying a visit, on the day after his arrival in the city, to 'the seminary, the women's prison of Giudecca, (and) the male prison of Santa Maria

Maggiore'.[9] Similarly, in the inaugural address which he worked on throughout the night after his election and which outlined the aims of his pontificate, John Paul I offered his greetings to various groups of people, including 'the suffering, the sick, *prisoners* ... those who are down on their luck' (italics added).

So far as prisoners are concerned, the attitude of the present Pope, John Paul II, might be described as the attitudes of his three predecessors writ large. Perhaps his own experience in a country deprived of its freedom has given him a special kinship with all those who, for whatever reason, have forfeited their liberty.

On a variety of occasions and in different parts of the world he has turned his attention to the imprisoned. During his visit to Mexico, for example, he declared: 'The Lord, in the final analysis, will identify himself with the disinherited, the sick, the *imprisoned* ... who have been given a helping hand' (italics added).

In his address to the Irish bishops in Dublin in 1979 he underscored their special obligations to men and women in prison. 'Bishops are called', he said, 'to be the fathers of all their people ... They should have a special care for those who live on the margin of society. Among those most needing pastoral care from bishops are prisoners ... do not neglect to provide for their spiritual needs and to concern yourselves also about their material conditions and their families.

'Have a special care for young offenders. So often their wayward lives are due to society's neglect more than to their own sinfulness. Detention should be especially for them a school of rehabilitation.'

A few months later, on the afternoon of the feast of Epiphany, he was putting those words into action. At a Juvenile Detention Centre in Rome, he listened to the youngsters as they strummed their guitars and often hummed the tunes himself: he prayed with them and spoke to them in their chapel. He reminded them of the text from Isaiah, which forms part of the liturgy of the feast: 'Arise, shine; for your light has come, and the glory of the Lord has risen upon you' (60:1). Then, he continued: 'Dear young men, awaken and rejoice because light has come for everyone ... His mercy and His love shine forth on each of us. I am happy to reflect with you on these truths because ... I know your problems. I understand your difficulties ... in particular how difficult it is for you to look to the future with confidence. However, I would like everyone of you to become aware of the strength that lies in your own life and which is able to blossom into a worthwhile future. I want to say to each of you that you have capacities for good, sometimes made even greater ... by your particularly hard experience of life. Be assured that I have come in your midst because I love you and have confidence in you ... If you should sometimes be seized by the sad thought that people look at you with eyes that humiliate and mortify, and that your dear ones do not have confidence in you, be assured that the Pope addresses you with esteem as young men who have the capacity to do much good in the future.'

John Paul II declared 1983 a special Holy Year, commemorating the 1,950th anniversary of the redeeming death of our Lord, and in November of that year he welcomed in the Sala Clementina a group of prison chaplains. He commented on the particular appropriateness of meeting them in 'The Jubilee Year of Redemption': ' ... I would like to express most sincerely the appreciation of the Church for the apostolate which you carry out. Beside you I see our brothers in jail. Those awaiting trial and those serving their sentence; those who count the days, anticipating the joys of freedom, as well as those others who see freedom only in the long distant future. I see the young and the old, men and women. I think about those who find themselves in prison for the first time and those who have become institutionalised. In your eyes I see reflected a world of suffering ... To all these brothers I send my profound and affectionate greetings. I am privileged in the name of Christ ... to convey to their hearts the ultimate certainty of God's love and merciful assistance. Such love is able to stoop to each prodigal son ... The ancient precept (about visiting the imprisoned) is more urgent than ever to-day. Christ identifies himself with the prisoner. This is a reality which you touch daily, but one needs to meditate constantly upon its inexhaustible richness ... '

As every chaplain knows, anyone who speaks about prisoners, and in particular anyone who has anything favourable to say about them, is likely to be told that he would quickly change his tune if he were to be on the receiving end of a robbery, of an act of personal violence or of some other crime. However, we knew that the Pope whom we listened to in the Sala Clementina was a man who had been on the receiving end of an assassination attempt only eighteen months previously. And just a month later, on 27 December 1983, he would be entering Rome's Rebibbia prison to seek out his would-be assassin and assure him that he had forgiven him. The pictures which appeared in newspapers and flashed across television screens, showing the Pope in deep conversation with Mehmet Ali Agca, were an eloquent portrayal of the gospel message of Christian compassion and forgiveness.

Later, in the prison chapel, John Paul II celebrated Mass and preached a homily in which he recalled to his listeners the words spoken by our Lord in the synagogue at Nazareth and reminded them that the 'glad tidings' which Jesus brings to men includes 'the release of prisoners'. He displayed great sensitivity as he addressed those prisoners just two days after Christmas. 'My encounter with you during this Christmas season', he said, 'moves me deeply. I can imagine what you are thinking: these are days in which the memory of our loved ones becomes more intense and the desire to be able to return to the intimacy of our own home floods our hearts with deep nostalgia. I can imagine it, and it was precisely for this reason that I decided to come to you within these walls which cannot but feel so foreign and cold to you, to bring you the warmth of a friendly word along with the comfort of an invitation to hope.

'I would like to be able to speak to each of you ... Above all, I would like to be able to listen to what each of you would like to tell me ... Unfortunately, this face-to-face encounter is not possible, but I would like each of you to listen to me as if my words were addressed to you alone.

'I try to imagine ... the desires which each of you carries in his heart. Many things which you desire, unfortunately are not in my power to grant you, as you well understand. Nevertheless, I feel that I do have something of great importance to give you. What I can give you above all, as a man and as a Christian, is respect. As priest and as bishop, I can offer you help to understand the meaning of this moment in your lives, a difficult moment but one which in its own way may nevertheless prove to be useful in preparing a better future.'

However, it was during his pastoral visit to Britain in 1982 that Pope John Paul II made perhaps his most significant statement about the relationship between priesthood and prison apostolate. It was at Heaton Park in Manchester. Before him were twelve young men about to be ordained. In the span of his brief address he wanted to outline for them – and for the whole Christian family – some of the vitally important aspects of the ministry about to be entrusted to them.

At this point, the reader might pause to reflect for a moment on what he would have included, had he been in the Pope's place at that moment. In particular would he have given even a thought to prisoners? This is part of what the Pope had to say: ' ... do not forget all those with special needs. Particularly those who are in prison and their families. In the Gospel Christ identifies himself with prisoners when he says "I was in prison and you visited me". And remember that he did not specify whether they were innocent or guilty.'

He could hardly have made the point more decisively. He was summarising the teaching and example of himself, of his predecessors and of Christian people throughout the ages; he was calling upon us all to return to our Christian sources and to recognise the unmistakable truth that the apostolate to the imprisoned has deep roots stretching back into the rich and fertile soil of the gospels.

3

PENAL HISTORY AND THE PRISON CHAPLAIN

The mood and temper of the public in regard to the treatment of crime and criminals is one of the most unfailing tests of the civilization of any country.

(Winston Churchill, 20 July 1910)

One of the most enjoyable ventures I was ever engaged in was the braille class. The pupils were eight or nine prisoner volunteers, the teachers two Sisters of Charity from the nearby School for the Blind, and the purpose of the class to help the prisoners to reach such brailling proficiency that they would be able to transcribe books and pamphlets for blind children.

In my purely supervisory capacity, I had plenty of opportunity to mix with the men, to listen to them and talk with them, and occasionally to overhear fascinating snatches of conversation. They were all very interested in the Sisters and in what they did. One day I heard Charlie asking his neighbour, Jimmie, who was regarded as pretty knowledgeable in religious matters because he attended chapel service every Sunday, to tell him something more about the Sisters. Gallantly, Jimmie launched into a brief account of what he knew about nuns, ending up with a reference to the three traditional vows. Charlie listened in silence. Then he said, 'Poverty? I've not gorra penny to me name! Chastity? Well, you can't 'ave a bird in 'ere, can you? Obedience? You've gorra obey, 'aven't you? Otherwise the screws would 'ave you'. After another brief pause he added pensively: 'You know, Jimmie, there really isn't much difference between them and us, is there? – 'cept of course *they* asked for it!'

As will become apparent, Charlie was rather nearer to the truth than he, or I, could have realised. At that time I knew as little about the history of prisons as he knew about the monastic life. But I was anxious to find out more. What I learned is to be the subject of this chapter. I hope it will introduce the reader to what has been happening in British prisons over the years and in particular give some indication of the work of prison chaplains.

For convenience, the story to be told can be divided into three sections: the period before 1877, when the Home Secretary took over responsibility for prisons in England and Wales, and the prison systems of Scotland and Ireland were similarly centralised; the first half of the twentieth century; and the period since the Second World War.

Key events (1)

1553 – The Bridewell, a former royal palace, given to the city of London by Edward VI as a 'workhouse for the poor and idle people'; the term 'bridewell' came to be applied to other workhouses and houses of correction

1593 – Beginning of transportation of convicted criminals to the American Colonies

1773 – Justices of the Peace empowered to appoint salaried chaplains to prisons

1776 – End of transportation to America

1777 – John Howard's report *The State of the Prisons in England and Wales* published

1813 – Elizabeth Fry's first visit to Newgate prison

1816 – Opening of Millbank, the first national penitentiary in England

1823 – Robert Peel's Gaol Act – first step towards general prison reform: obliged local authorities to implement many of John Howard's proposed reforms

1835 – Appointment by Home Secretary of Inspectors of Prisons who were to visit and report on all prisons

1838 – Parkhurst Military Hospital on the Isle of Wight opens as first prison for juveniles

1842 – Opening of Pentonville Model Prison, London

1850 – Central government assumed control of the convict prison service

1857 – All transportation officially ended, though in fact it continued for another decade

1863 – Local magistrates empowered to appoint and pay Roman Catholic and Methodist clergy as prison chaplains
     – A House of Lords Committee on gaol discipline recommended 'hard labour, hard fare and hard bed'

1865 – Prison Act aimed at securing uniformity of treatment; gaols and houses of correction amalgamated, and designated 'local prisons'; provision of single cells for each prisoner

1877 – Control of all prisons in England and Wales vested in Home Secretary

Prisons seem to be as old as the human race. There are endless references to them in the Bible, from the first book, Genesis, where the unhappy

Joseph is imprisoned in Egypt (Gen 39:20ff.), to the last book, Revelation, where John is condemned to the equivalent of prison by being banished to the tiny island of Patmos off the coast of modern Turkey (Rev 1:9).

But though prisons have always been with us, it is only during the past two hundred years that they have served a punitive function. Before that, they were used almost exclusively either as a means of coercing debtors, or as a kind of waiting room where suspects were held pending their trial and the guilty pending execution of sentence. The only major exceptions were the bridewells, or houses of correction, which were set up in Tudor times to deal with petty criminals and others deemed to be on the fringes of crime, such as the destitute. The inmates were submitted to a regime which was intended not only to punish but also to reform, and so the bridewells 'can truly be treated as the first example of modern imprisonment – certainly in Britain and probably in Europe'.[1]

Eventually the houses of correction became indistinguishable from the common gaols which were under the control of the county sheriffs. The sheriffs appointed others to run them, and, since wages were not provided, the gaolers had to use their own entrepreneurial skills. They levied fees not only on release, and on every possible occasion during the course of a sentence (e.g. to exchange heavy fetters for lighter ones), but even on entry. Indeed, in the Fleet prison immortalised by Dickens, where charges were on a sliding scale, an imprisoned Archbishop was expected to offer an entrance fee of £10![2]

Conditions in these local gaols were appalling; as many as one in four prisoners died each year of gaol fever. It was when John Howard became High Sheriff of Bedfordshire and discovered at first hand the misery and squalor in his own county gaol that he resolved to devote his considerable energies to prison reform. If, as mentioned in the last chapter, he made most of his long tours on horseback that was because, after even a few hours in the fetid atmosphere of a gaol, he could not bear to sit in a coach with the prison stench still clinging to his clothes. The recommendations he made are in themselves an indication of what gaols were like in eighteenth-century England. He urged, for example, that there should be separation of men from women, that prison walls should be scraped and whitewashed annually, that gaolers should be paid and fee-taking abolished, that useful labour should be introduced and the sale of liquor prohibited.

The kinds of punishment that awaited those guilty of minor crimes were the stocks, the pillory, or a flogging: even women were flogged in public until early in the nineteenth century. But the State knew of only one way of dealing with serious crime, and that was by removing its perpetrators from the scene – either to the New World by transportation, or to the Next World by the death penalty. Such penalties were inflicted not only on adults, but on children too. Up to 1868 executions took on the appearance of a public fiesta, and one historian notes that at the gallows at Tyburn 'a girl and a boy might be seen dangling between a highwayman and a murderer'.[3] To this day it is an awesome experience to visit the group of cells in Parkhurst prison whose doorways are unusually low because in those cells in days gone by youngsters were held while they awaited transportation across the oceans.

However, just before John Howard's book *The State of the Prisons in England and Wales* appeared, the Declaration of Independence robbed England of its convict colonies in America, and ushered in the era of the 'hulks'. Prisoners, otherwise due for transportation, were housed in ships moored in the Thames or the Medway under conditions of overcrowding and filth even worse than those in the local gaols, and each day they were employed in harsh public works, such as the dredging of rivers. Even though these floating prisons were to continue in existence for many years, and even though new sites for transportation were to become available for a time in Australia, it was clear that land-based prisons would have to be built. The need for such institutions was put beyond question by the sharp reduction in the number of categories of crime that could be visited with the death penalty: by early in the nineteenth century these categories had dropped from well over 200 to a mere handful. Prisons could no longer serve simply as a stepping stone, as had usually been the case in the past, to transportation or the death penalty. Instead, prison itself, with the loss of freedom it entailed, would be the penalty. Imprisonment in the modern sense of the word had come into existence.

In 1816 the national Penitentiary of Millbank, erected on the site now partly occupied by the Tate Gallery, opened its gates for the first batch of prisoners. It was so huge and complex that one old warder, who spent most of his adult life there, had to carry a piece of chalk 'with which he "blazed" his path as the American backwoodsman does the forest trees'.[4] Other prisons followed at Parkhurst, Portland and Dartmoor, and then, in 1842, Pentonville Prison was opened. It was called the Model Prison, the first of a series of over fifty prison buildings that were constructed on similar lines during the next few years, and which still remain in use in the last quarter of the twentieth century. In 1850 the small group of prisons, including those mentioned in this paragraph, which were used by central government to house 'convicts', i.e. those awaiting transportation or serving the new sentence of penal servitude instead of being transported, were placed under the control of the Directors of Convict Prisons.

It has been suggested that prison as we know it today stems from a monograph written by a seventeenth-century Benedictine monk, in which he recommends that wrongdoers be reformed by sampling a spell of monastic life. Whatever truth in that suggestion, it is undeniable that the penal institutions which arose here and in the United States bear a superficial likeness to a monastery. Their inhabitants live behind walls, in cells, and follow a life of poverty, chastity and obedience – without the option. They have with justification been described as 'Reluctant Monks'.

Various possible penal regimes were proposed and hotly discussed: one allowed convicts to work together but insisted on total silence at all times. (This gave rise to a highly developed range of non-verbal communication among prisoners: by touching the side of his nose, for example, a man was signalling his interest in 'snout', the prison argot for tobacco.) Another regime did not even allow associated work; during exercise periods the prisoners wore hoods and when they attended chapels sat in cubicle-like stalls which enabled them to see no one but the preacher and the warders. The great aim was to prevent contamination and to deter. But there was also a belief in the spiritual value of silence which would have done credit to a community of Carthusian monks. Indeed, it was fondly believed in some quarters that if you left a prisoner long enough in his own cell in utter silence and with a Bible in his hand, he would eventually see the light. In fact, many of those subjected to such treatment ended up insane.

Given the quasi-monastic character of prisons, it is perhaps not too surprising that one of the few positive discoveries made by John Howard was that chaplains had been appointed to most of the county gaols. In the course of the next century the status of the prison chaplain ranked next only to that of the governor, and on occasion seemed almost to surpass it. Not only was the chaplain's hierarchical position enshrined in legislation – an Act of 1877 numbered the chaplain, together with the governor and medical officer, as one of the 'superior officers' – but it was also in a sense built into the very architecture of many of the prisons where there was 'only one entrance which was usually flanked by the governor's house on one side, and the chaplain's on the other'.[5] One of the first prison inspectors had earlier been chaplain of Millbank, and his successor, the Reverend Daniel Nihil, was appointed Chaplain-Governor of the same establishment. This combination of roles was never to be repeated, but while it lasted warders often carried Bibles with them in ostentatious fashion and could usually be relied upon to provide, at the turn of a key, an apt scriptural quotation. And even when the roles were separated, there was still considerable confidence in the reformatory value of religion.

That is not to say that at times chaplains did not err by way of excess in their evangelistic fervour. A prisoner, writing in the *Newgate Monthly Magazine* at about the time that Elizabeth Fry was a frequent visitor to the prison, recalls the grim event which occurred on the Sunday before each batch of executions. There would be almost a hundred per cent attendance to hear the condemned sermon and to gaze upon the men in the condemned pew, an oval-shaped, sable-coloured box large enough to contain thirty persons: a coffin lay on a table in the middle and with this bizarre visual aid before them, they were reminded by the chaplain that 'they would in all probability never hear another sermon'. The prisoner, appalled by the insensitivity of the whole event, goes on to speak of the indignation he felt when 'next morning at half-past seven the clergyman's voice was heard in the vaulting passages, "I am the resurrection and the life"'.[6]

In all truth, the chaplains were assigned a bewildering range of tasks. In addition to their predictable religious duties – preaching, recitation of daily prayers, celebration of holy communion, religious instruction, visiting cells, attending those in the condemned cell – they were obliged by prison rules to observe the mental condition of prisoners, to keep a character book and a journal of events, distribute books and other educational material, superintend the schools, supervise all welfare activities; in many prisons they were also expected to act as entertainment officers and librarians.[7]

Their annual reports give us a dramatic glimpse into prison life at this time, and were frequently used by chaplains as a way of trying to influence penal policy. Some of these clerics, like the Reverend John Clay who was chaplain at Preston prison for over thirty years, even made forays into what would nowadays be called criminology. Another chaplain, who believed that alcohol was the root of all evil, invented a 'beerometer' by which he proved, at least to his own satisfaction, that the rise and fall in the prison population was a precise reflection of the amount of beer consumed by the community outside.[8]

However, despite the occasional excess or eccentricity, nothing can diminish the immense contribution made by chaplains in the hundred years up to 1877, sometimes quite heroically, as when they laboured in the hulks, in 'the worst conditions imaginable this side of hell'. Those hundred years might not unfairly be summarised as a period in which the ideals of John Howard were gradually implemented. A series of Acts aimed to ensure the proper inspection of prisons and a uniform policy throughout the system. All the efforts of the century, however, finally culminated in 1877 in the passing of an Act of Parliament which transferred all prisons into the control of the Home Secretary. This event marked a turning point in penal history – the end of the beginning of the modern prison system.

Throughout this period the history of Scottish and Irish prisons was broadly the same as that in England and Wales: their provision and control remained a local responsibility until the nineteenth century; then an element of central inspection emerged (in Ireland some ten years earlier than in England and Scotland) and with it greater uniformity; and finally in 1877 the two prison systems were fully centralised, the administration of prisons becoming the task of the Scottish Prison Commission and General Prison Board for Ireland. (Shortly after 1920 the prisons in Northern Ireland became the direct responsibility of the Ministry of Home Affairs, a situation which continued until 1972 when that responsibility passed to the Secretary of State for Northern Ireland.)

Key events (2)

1878 – Implementation of Prison Act (1877) and setting up of Prison Commission
1881 – First report of the Commissioners
1895 – The Gladstone Report
1898 – Prison Act to implement the Report
     – The convict prison service and the local prison service amalgamated
1907 – Setting up of the Probation Service
1908 – Borstal detention begins; juvenile courts established
1910 – Winston Churchill, Home Secretary, reduces prison population; gives famous speech in which he insists that a society's 'civilisation' can be gauged by its treatment of prisoners
1922 – Alexander Paterson becomes a Commissioner: beginning of the Golden Age of prison and borstal systems
     – Publication of *English Prisons Today*, a highly critical report written by S. Hobhouse and A. Fenner Brockway, who had had first-hand experience of prison as conscientious objectors in the First World War
1930 – First open borstal at Lowdham Grange, Nottinghamshire
1932 – Reformatories renamed Approved Schools
1936 – First adult open prison at New Hall Camp, West Yorkshire
1938 – The Prison Officers' Association officially approved

It was on 4 April 1878 that the first great act of nationalisation took place: all local prisons in England and Wales became the responsibility of central government. At the same time the Prison Commission came into existence, the agency through which the Home Secretary would exercise control over penal establishments. Its first chairman Sir Edmund du Cane had no doubts about the twin objectives that he and his three fellow commissioners should pursue: first, 'a uniform system of punishment' aimed at the repression of crime, which, he explained, 'is the great object of punishment'; and, second, 'economy in the expenses of prisons'. By immediately closing over a quarter of the 113 local prisons placed in their charge, the Commissioners gave notice that they meant business. It soon became evident that this was to be so not only on the economic front but on the prison regime front also. For far too long gross inequalities had existed between the conditions in one prison and those in another: a Speaker in the House of Commons had picturesquely remarked that: 'a harlequin's jacket is a consistent colour in comparison'.

It was to the credit of the Commissioners, therefore, that within three years they were able to report that throughout the land uniformity of discipline and diet had been achieved, prison sanitation improved and a 'stage system' introduced, which enabled prisoners to earn increased privileges and decreased severity as a reward for good behaviour.

Nonetheless, it comes as something of a shock to learn that it was not until a man had progressed to the fourth and final stage that he was allowed to write or receive letters, or to have visits from his wife or parents.

Though the chaplains no longer enjoyed the high status that they had known in the first three quarters of the century and though the area of their work had begun to contract – a few years earlier a chaplain had judged it part of his brief to act as a kind of sanitary inspector, using his annual report to comment on the plumbing arrangements in his establishment – they still were held in considerable esteem, and religious education was regarded as a central feature of the prison regime. Du Cane himself wrote with some enthusiasm of the ministry of the chaplains, little realising that before long a chaplain would become one of his most bitter critics.

Despite their undoubted successes, the Commissioners acted with considerable ruthlessness and inflexibility. One penal historian maintains that Du Cane instituted 'the most blatantly deterrent regime ever instituted in British prisons'.[9] 'In place of filth, jail fever and corruption', comments a keen observer of the Victorian scene, 'came the treadmill, the crank and strict regimentation.'[10] It was said that a Commissioner could stand, watch in hand, at any hour of the day and know what was happening at that particular time in any local prison in the country. As for types of labour, the crank consisted of a heavy handle which a prisoner would turn for so many revolutions, in a drum filled with sand or gravel or some other resistant material; the tightening of a screw on the crank made it still more difficult to turn and led to the nickname 'screws' being applied to those who did the tightening, the prison warders or officers. The treadmill was usually set in a stall where the prisoner revolved a wheel by the pressure of his weight upon the steps beneath his feet. A warder of the 1850s explained how it worked: 'You see, the men can get no firm tread like, from the steps always sinking away from under their feet and *that* makes it very tiring'.[11] Indeed, it did. Some treadmills served a useful purpose – like that at Durham prison which pumped water from a well, or the huge sixty-man treadmill at Shepton Mallet which provided energy for a nearby corn-mill – but for the most part they, like the cranks, did no more than offer, in the words of Du Cane, 'hard, dull, useless, uninteresting, monotonous labour'. Even more dreaded than either crank or treadmill was the infamous 'shot-drill' which involved the prisoners in the aimless and back-breaking task of carrying 28-pound cannon-balls around from one point to another.

By the 1890s there was considerable public disquiet about the state of the prisons, a disquiet increased by a press campaign in which the Reverend Dr William Morrison, chaplain of Wandsworth prison, played a notable part. He claimed that the repressive measures of Du Cane, far from leading to a reduction in crime, had exactly the opposite effect.

This attack finally persuaded the Home Secretary to order an official enquiry under the presidency of Mr Herbert Gladstone. Within twelve months the Gladstone Committee had published its report, 'the Magna Carta' as it has been called, 'of the British penal system'. It went to the heart of the problem – over-centralisation. Though much attention had been given to organisation, finance, statistics, even prisoners' health, 'the prisoners (themselves) have been treated too much as a hopeless and worthless element of the community'. It also pinpointed the remedy: 'We think that the system should be made more elastic, more capable of being adapted to the special cases of individual prisoners', and prison discipline should have as its aim 'to maintain, stimulate or awaken the higher susceptibilities of prisoners ... and wherever possible to turn them out of prison better men and women physically and morally than when they came in'. Furthermore, the Report enunciated the famous principle 'that prison treatment should have as its primary and *concurrent* objects, deterrence and reform' (italics added), a principle which was to guide prison developments for the best part of the twentieth century.

The Prison Act of 1898, incorporating many of the Committee's recommendations, abolished the treadwheel, the crank and other forms of unproductive labour; it reduced solitary confinement; it restricted the use of corporal punishment; it introduced remission, as well as special classification and separate accommodation of first offenders, juveniles and habitual criminals. All this was a far cry from the 'hard labour, hard fare, hard bed' regime that had been advocated by a select committee of the House of Lords thirty years earlier.

In the year the Gladstone Report appeared, Du Cane had retired and was succeeded by Sir Evelyn Ruggles-Brise. Under his leadership many improvements were effected in prison conditions, including the introduction of the weekly, as opposed to the fortnightly, bath for all inmates! More importantly, there were statutory provisions aimed at keeping people out of prison, like the setting up of the Probation Service in 1907 and, in the following year, a Children's Act which prohibited imprisonment for the under-fourteens and limited it for youngsters between fourteen and sixteen. For many years chaplains had been concerned about the plight of children in prison – the report of the Roman Catholic priest in Durham shows that in one year alone he wrote almost 300 letters to the parents of juveniles in his care begging them to look after their children on their release[12] – and increasingly joined governors in voicing their anxieties. They must have rejoiced, then, when in 1908 the courts were given power to pass a sentence of detention in a Borstal Institution for offenders between sixteen and twenty-one as an alternative to imprisonment. This new provision was the brainchild of the Chairman of the Commissioners who had already experimented with special training institutions for the young. It is to the first of those institutions, set up in the village of Borstal, Kent, in 1902, that the borstal system owed its name.

Just as chaplains had worked in the hulks and the local prisons, so now they began to work in the borstals, and every encouragement was given them. They still retained primary responsibility for education and for libraries, and there is a modern ring in the words of the chaplain of Aylesbury borstal for girls when he plaintively reports: 'The library books are in good order, but ... works of fiction, generally regarded as masterpieces, make no appeal to them at all ... They enquire for two types of works, viz. "about love" or "about murder" with a marked preference for murder'.[13]

The borstal system was perhaps the most outstanding achievement of Ruggles-Brise but it was by no means his only one. Yet, despite penological advances, there were also setbacks and a tendency to return to harshness and inflexibility.

At Rochester Youth Custody Centre there is the record of a fascinating correspondence between the governor and one of the Commissioners, which shows that even at the turn of the century penal institutions were as 'closed' to the world at large as any enclosed order of monks might be. He complains to the Commissioner that the chaplain had informed inmates of the death of Queen Victoria, an action which he himself as governor would not have been allowed to do. The Commissioner replies that he has been in touch with the offending chaplain and is confident that there will be no further indiscretions. But, not very long after, the governor complains that the chaplain 'has done it again'. Albeit in the context of a sermon against the evils of gambling, he writes, the chaplain ought not to have given the prisoners the name of the winner of the Grand National!

When a report on prison conditions which had been sponsored by the Labour Party appeared in 1922, the year after Ruggles-Brise's retirement, its authors, who had sampled prison as conscientious objectors, concluded: 'making every allowance for the slow and cautious development by the Commissioners of certain recommendations of the Gladstone Committee, the principles and effects of their regime were scarcely distinguishable from those of the Du Cane regime'.[14]

Perhaps history will be more generous in its assessment of Ruggles-Brise. It is scarcely likely to alter the handsome tributes that, even during his lifetime, were paid to Commissioner Sir Alexander Paterson. Though never the Chairman of the Prison Commission, and though on joining the Commission at the age of thirty-eight he was younger than any governor in the system, he was to dominate the prison scene for the next quarter of a century. At the time of his death it was reported: 'To his imagination and inventive force we owe almost all the schemes of penal reform which have been developed in this country in the last twenty-five years'.[15] Paterson's interest in prisons had begun at least a decade earlier, when he had visited a young Bermondsey lad who had been sentenced to penal servitude in Dartmoor prison for murdering his wife. He has left a vivid description of his impressions: 'As I walked along the endless landings and corridors in the great cellular blocks, I saw something of the 1,500 men who were then immured in Dartmoor. Their drab uniforms were plastered with broad arrows, their heads were closely shaven ... Not even a safety razor was allowed, so that in addition to the stubble on their heads, their faces were covered with a sort of dirty moss ... The prison regime, resting primarily on considerations of safe custody and security, had succeeded in making a large number of human beings objects of contempt. No child could have recognised his father in such a condition, no girl or wife believe she ever loved a man who looked like that.'[16]

In the light of these remarks it is not surprising that among the reforms associated with Paterson were: the virtual disappearance of the silence rule; the abolition of the convict's crop and broad-arrow clothing; the organisation of shaving facilities; the provision of better visiting and exercise arrangements; the attempt to provide eight hours of work for every prisoner and the introduction of an earnings scheme; the removal of prison officers (since 1921 they had ceased to be called 'warders') to the back and sides of the chapels where they could be members of the worshipping community, instead of being perched on high seats facing the congregation, as had formerly been the practice.

Perhaps Paterson's boldest initiative, however, was the setting up of the first *open* borstals and prisons in the 1930s. It was as though he was attempting to resolve the paradox that he himself had pointed to when he had written that 'you cannot train men for freedom in a condition of captivity'. (Scotland followed England's example in 1953 by opening its first open prison.) To Paterson, also, goes the credit for the oft-quoted saying that 'men come to prison as a punishment not for punishment' – as a punishment, and therefore conditions must not be made too attractive, but not for punishment and, therefore, there is no justification for deliberately allowing bad conditions to persist for the purpose of deterrence.

Alexander Paterson's influence upon penal reform was summed up by Sir Lionel Fox, one-time Chairman of the Prison Commission, when he spoke of Paterson as having 'breathed life into the honoured formulae of the Gladstone Report' and when he singled out among Paterson's most valuable contributions 'his insistence that it is through men and not through buildings or regulations that this work must be done; his flair for finding the right men to do it; and his ability to inspire them with his own faith'.

The Paterson era has with some justification been described as the Golden Age of the prison and borstal systems in England and Wales. The borstals especially, with their public school ethos – one judge is reputed to have said that a borstal sentence was the equivalent of a free place at

Eton – and their allegedly remarkable success rate, made them the envy of other countries. As the fourth decade of the twentieth century drew to a close, the enthusiasm and the confidence, though waning a little perhaps, persisted until 1939, when Europe was plunged into a war which left very little time or energy for consideration of prisons and prisoners. Many inmates nearing the end of their sentences got an early release and joined the armed forces. Some of them continued to write to the chaplains whom they had known in prison. I wonder if any of them wrote so honestly as the ex-prisoner in the 1914–18 War who in a Christmas letter to his chaplain friend had admitted: 'I am trying to do my best for my King and country, although I am a bit of a devil when I am drunk'![17]

Key events (3)

1948 – The Criminal Justice Act (1)
1949 – The Prison Rules
1950 – Chaplain Inspector at headquarters [see Appendix A for further information about structure of Chaplaincy]
1959 – White Paper: *Penal Practice in a Changing Society*
1961 – The Criminal Justice Act (2)
1962 – Opening of the first (and still the only) psychiatric prison at Grendon Underwood, Bucks
1963 – The Prison Commission merged into the Home Office
1965 – Great Train Robbery
1966 – The Mountbatten Report
1967 – The Criminal Justice Act (3)
1968 – The Radzinowicz Report – beginning of dispersal system
1969 – White Paper: *People in Prison*; Abolition of death penalty; Children and Young Persons Act
1972 – The Criminal Justice Act (4)
1979 – The May Report
1980 – Prison Officers' dispute begins
1982 – The Criminal Justice Act (5)
1983 – Initiation of massive prison building programme

The four decades since the war have been punctuated by no less than five Criminal Justice Acts, each leaving its mark on the penal scene. The first of them had been ready for presentation to Parliament in 1938 but the advent of war led to its being shelved for ten years.

When this Act did appear – and a similar one in Scotland the following year – it seemed that the reformative ideals of the Gladstone Report were at last being brought to fruition. Liberal-minded people rejoiced at many of the Act's provisions: the abolition of the use of the cat-o'-nine tails (the final abandonment of corporal punishment in prison did not occur until the Criminal Justice Act of 1967 banned the use of the birch); the introduction of measures to reduce the possibility of imprisonment for juveniles, the mentally disordered and first offenders; and the setting up of detention centres which would give a 'short, sharp shock' to youngsters and thereby, it was hoped, deter them from deeper involvement in criminal activities.

The revised Prison Rules which appeared the following year adopted an optimistic approach: Rule Six, which was later to be promoted to Rule One because it seemed to epitomise what prison is all about, boldly declares: 'The purpose of the training and treatment of convicted prisoners shall be to encourage and assist them to lead a good and useful life'. Indeed, during the first decade or so after the war, there was a general spirit of optimism in the Prison Service, a belief that there would be continuing progress, a conviction that prison could reform adults just as borstals apparently reformed youngsters. In fact, at the end of the sixties the Home Office was encouraging the Courts not to give short sentences, since they allowed insufficient time for the reformative influences of prison to take effect.[18]

Immense effort was put into the preparation and running of programmes geared to the reform of those in custody. Education of a remedial and more advanced kind was promoted; so too was group therapy and the employment of officers in work of a social nature for prisoners. The arrival on the scene of assistant governors and prison welfare officers was welcomed as a means of enhancing the rehabilitative effectiveness of imprisonment. So far as work was concerned, the Commissioners were able to report in the mid-fifties that over the course of several years no prisoners had been unemployed and many of them had had a full working week.

However, a White Paper of 1959 carried the cautionary title *Penal Practice in a Changing Society*. Changes in society there certainly were, but already there were signs of even more dramatic changes within the penal system itself. Less than four years after the White Paper, the Prison Commission was disbanded and, in accordance with the Criminal Justice Act of 1961, full responsibility for prisons and borstals was transferred to a Department of the Home Office. (In Scotland a similar change had taken place thirty-five years earlier when the Scottish Prisons Commission was replaced by a Prisons Department.) The change, it was argued, would make it patently clear that the Home Secretary was fully responsible for the whole criminal justice system and enable him to tackle existing problems more effectively. Not everyone was, or is, impressed by the reasons given for the disappearance of the Prison Commissioners and their replacement by a more impersonal Department of State. It was a chaplain who had served both before and after 1963 who remarked with nostalgia, and some hyperbole: 'It is like the changeover from a cottage industry to a giant bureaucracy, and I don't known who – if anybody – is going to benefit from it'.

In 1957 Harold Macmillan might declare that 'most of our people have never had it so good', but in the Prison Service that was far from being the case. True, for a while during the fifties the number of people in prison had begun to drop in a most encouraging way, but soon it recommenced its upward trend and within ten years it had reached a new peak and was continuing to rise. Between the wars the prison population had hovered around the 11,000 mark, but in 1966 it was more than three times, and in 1977 almost four times, that figure. And all this despite the fact that the Criminal Justice Acts of 1967 and 1972 had provided alternatives to custodial sentences (such as suspended sentences, community service orders and day training centres), and, by the introduction of parole, had made possible the reduction of up to two-thirds of the length of sentences served by many prisoners.

Developments in the criminal justice systems of England, Scotland and Northern Ireland followed rather different paths. Thus, no provision was made in Scotland for suspended sentences or for day training centres, nor, in Northern Ireland, for detention centres or a parole system either; however, there was in the Province an entitlement to one-half remission as opposed to one-third in the other two countries. Despite these minor differences, the general aim throughout the United Kingdom was the same: to keep people out of prison by finding alternatives to custodial sentences; and, unhappily, the result was the same also: a relentless increase in the number of men, women and youngsters in prison. In Scotland the number rose from about 1,500 in 1938 to over 5,000 in 1972, and in Northern Ireland, where as late as 1966 it was still under 500, there occurred the most extraordinary increase of all, as tragic events in the Province sent the prison population soaring to almost 3,000, a 600 per cent increase by 1978. (In the Irish Republic also a similar pattern emerged: in 1961 the daily average number of convicted prisoners was under 450, by 1981 it was almost 2,000.[19])

Not only were the prisons overcrowded, they were for the most part very old and in desperate need of refurbishing. What the Prison Department had inherited in 1963 made it, as one writer puts it, 'a major slum landlord',[20] and in those slum conditions prisoners had to live and prison officers work. Though some former military camps were converted into penal establishments and a number of new prisons built, including Grendon psychiatric prison (once described as 'the brightest jewel in the prison system') and the first industrial prison at Coldingley, it was still impossible to keep pace with the relentless pressure imposed on the system.

To add to the troubles, a spate of escapes, culminating in that of the notorious spy George Blake from Wormwood Scrubs in 1966, made it clear that too many prisons were not only old and overcrowded, they were also frighteningly vulnerable. Earl Mountbatten was commissioned to head an enquiry into the question of prison security. In an amazingly brief period of under four months the Mountbatten Report was completed. It concluded that there was no really secure prison in the country, and indicated how this state of affairs might be remedied. It called for the classification of all prisoners into one of four categories, running from Category A (for those whose escape would be highly dangerous to the public or the police or to the security of the state) to Category D (for those who could be trusted in open conditions). It also recommended that the most dangerous prisoners should all be held in one high-security prison on the Isle of Wight, a kind of British Alcatraz. In the event the government of the day chose to follow the advice of a sub-committee of the Advisory Council on the Penal System in 1968 headed by Professor Leon Radzinowicz and, instead of concentrating dangerous prisoners in a single institution, decided to disperse them between several prisons.

However, most of the Mountbatten recommendations were implemented: the era of security officers and patrolling dogs and control rooms, of secure perimeters and floodlighting and electronic anti-escape devices had arrived. With it came that concern with security which has preoccupied the Prison Service ever since and swallowed up so many precious resources of men and money. On more than one occasion, and sometimes by the most unexpected people, I have been reminded of Shakespeare's warning: 'Security is mortals' chiefest enemy'.[21] But whatever excesses there may have been, there is no doubt that the tightening up of prison security came just in time: the sixties saw an increase in the number of sophisticated criminals, including many, such as the 'Great Train Robbers', who were serving very long sentences, and soon the Prison Service would have to deal with highly motivated terrorists.

At the end of the decade another White Paper was published which, according to at least one expert, 'may ... mark the end, in England, of the whole penological era which began with the publication of the Gladstone Report in 1895'. *People in Prison* sees 'the protection of society' as the over-riding purpose of imprisonment, and, for the first time, introduces the concept of prison as 'humane containment', a sterile concept which seems to reduce prison to the status of a 'cloakroom' (to quote Paterson) or a 'warehouse' (to quote Hall-Williams) where inmates are kept, albeit humanely, until their release.

As well as providing the White Paper, the year 1969 also brought the permanent abolition of capital punishment for murder. It was a decision widely welcomed by chaplains. Many of them had already expressed concern about the continued use of the death penalty, which they found difficult to reconcile with gospel values. Many, too, were relieved that they would no longer be called upon to minister in the death cells. It was a painful ordeal to visit a prisoner daily throughout the period that had to elapse between sentence and its execution, and then witness the untimely death of someone who had often become as close as a friend.

In the office of the Roman Catholic Chaplain of Strangeways Prison, Manchester, there is a crucifix, and beneath it a notice which explains that, in response to the request of a Catholic prisoner, the crucifix had been placed in the death cell, and had subsequently been returned there whenever a condemned prisoner asked for it. It is difficult to look at that crucifix without thinking of the men who in the last moments of their lives gazed upon the figure of their crucified Lord and of the chaplains who encouraged them to unite their deaths with His.

Inevitably, changes in the prison world, like changes in the world at large and changes in the Christian Churches themselves, had their implications for chaplains too. As long ago as 1951, the Commissioner Lionel Fox began his chapter on the Chaplain's Department, in his classic work *The English Prison and Borstal Systems*, by quoting with approval these words of Dr Max Grunhut: 'the better part of what has been done for prisoners beyond the maintenance of a marginal existence and the provision of work originated in pastoral work. Education and welfare work in prison – even more than in the world at large – are a secularisation of tasks undertaken originally by the Church and her ministers. The prison chaplain's original importance was that he was the one neutral force in an otherwise impersonal and repressive regime'.[22] But it is significant that he not only recognises that the chaplain has had to retreat from certain areas which were formerly his preserve but also hints at more radical changes to come. The past thirty years have proved the validity of his assessment.

The chief catalyst within the Prison Department which brought about this change in the role of the chaplain was the galaxy of 'specialists' who appeared in the penal firmament after World War II. Whereas in earlier days governor, chaplain and medical officer had been the undisputed triumvirate in every institution, now there were also assistant governors and probation officers, and education officers, and psychologists.[23] The Prison Act (1952) and the Prisons Rules (revised in 1964) might reaffirm the statutory position of the chaplain, but they could not always ease his fears that he was being pushed to the margins of prison life, that areas formerly his own were being wrested from him, that his own role was being called into question.

In the late sixties chapel-going ceased to be a compulsory activity for adult prisoners, and a few years later for young prisoners too. The chaplains themselves had advocated this change of policy – most of them would have applauded the sentiments if not the theology of the old lag who was placed on report for writing on his mug: 'Your order is for me to go to chapel, but mine is that I'll go to hell first'[24] – but the view was by no means unanimous. One chaplain, at a public meeting convened to discuss voluntary chapel attendance, roundly declared: 'England won't stand for this!' But of course England did. Less hysterically, most chaplains, while supporting the change in principle, were genuinely concerned about its effect on prisoners who found themselves having to 'opt-in' positively to chapel-going, often in the face of peer-group pressure. In fact chapel attendances remained extraordinary high in some institutions – even today they often run into hundreds in the bigger prisons – but in others they slumped pathetically.

In a sense the Chaplaincy was going through a paschal-like experience, a dying and a rising. For with hindsight it is not difficult to see that the traumas of the fifties and the sixties had their positive sides too. Despite initial misgivings, chaplains came not only to recognise the value of the contributions that others made to the welfare of prisoners, but also in many instances to develop with them a high degree of sharing and team work. The chaplains themselves, who had so often gone about their task in isolation in their individual institutions, began to grow into a chaplaincy, a unified and cohesive body, with a strong leadership and with more support for the men 'in the field'. They received better training – my own initiation into prison work had consisted of being dropped in at the deep end after just two brief sessions with my predecessor – they became more professional, in the sense of being more competent and more confident in the work they were called to do.

There were two other supremely important gains that emerged from the uncertainties and anxieties, the small 'deaths' that the Prison Chaplaincy had experienced. The first was a slow but continuing growth in ecumenical relationships between the Anglican, Roman Catholic and Methodist chaplains who are appointed to every institution. (In addition to these chaplains, visiting ministers of ethnic and minority faiths are also provided wherever they are needed. All the basic religious requirements of the adherents of these faiths, e.g. holy books, are always met. Requests for additional or more elaborate provisions are also met whenever it is reasonably possible to do so.) The other was that as chaplains forfeited much of their former status, the Church in prison saw the opportunity of becoming a Church like its Master, seeking 'not to be served, but to serve'; as chaplains gave up so many of the anomalous tasks which had accrued to them over the years – even a few years ago it was not unusual for them to act as entertainment officers – they were better able to reveal their true role as chaplains and that role, as the Chaplain General explained in 1973, is that we should be priests, pastors and prophets to prisoners and to staff. If that role was secured, what reason to hanker after the past?

As we have already seen, chaplains were by no means alone in passing through difficult times. For the whole Prison Service the sixties had been a traumatic decade, but there was worse to come. In the first place, a wave of prison riots and demonstrations began in Parkhurst in 1969, affected over forty establishments in 1972 and erupted in the fearful Hull riot of 1976 when three-quarters of a million pounds worth of damage was done. Second, overcrowding became even more severe, as the prison population continued to rise and as rioting took valuable accommodation out of use for months on end. In the 1980 annual report the Director

General of the Prison Service described the conditions in large areas of the penal system as 'an affront to a civilized society' (§11). His Deputy spoke with equal vigour, when, in the same report, he made the stinging comment that 'the Prison Service has become used to tolerating the intolerable' (§25).

In the third place, doubts were beginning to emerge about the real purpose of imprisonment. Since the Gladstone Report of 1895, reform had always been seen as an essential ingredient, even the key ingredient, of that purpose. But in 1977 an official review by the Home Office, *Prison and Prisoners*, accepted that 'research findings give little support to the view that imprisonment can directly alter the long term behaviour of prisoners'. Fourthly, there was among prison officers an increasing unrest, a loss of job-satisfaction, a feeling that they were misunderstood by the community at large, a belief that more concern was shown for prisoners than for themselves. It surfaced in the form of pay-demands, which were accompanied by widespread industrial action, including partial withdrawal of labour and eventually the bringing into use of old army camps and even of some army personnel to guard them.

In the face of this crisis Merlyn Rees set up a Committee under Mr Justice May to enquire into the state of the Prison Services in the United Kingdom. If the May Report did not prove to be what many had hoped for, 'a Gladstone Report for the twentieth century', it has nonetheless been far-reaching in its effects. In its more than 150 recommendations it not only goes into great detail about the pay and allowances of prison officers, but also advocates changes in the Prison Department in order to ensure greater openness, stricter accountability, more effective power in the regions and in individual institutions, and a growth in the sense of unity and identity. But for chaplains, especially, its most significant statements concern the very purpose and ethos of prisons. It claims that there is a 'moral vacuum' in the penal system, which is perhaps what a prison chaplain had in mind when he suggested that the Service 'has lost its soul'. It argues that Rule One, despite 'all the admirable and constructive things that are done in its name' has become more 'rhetoric' than 'reality'. Though prisons in themselves do not reform, they must be 'purposive communities' and those who work in them must have worthy and achievable goals set before them. Those goals, it suggests, might be described, in a kind of shorthand, as 'positive custody' – something more than 'containment', however 'humane' – a custody which respects the human dignity of prisoners and offers them opportunities for realising their potentialities.

The May Report seems finally to have laid to rest the reformative ideal which inspired so much that happened in prisons throughout the century; and it is not without significance that when the last of the five Criminal Justice Acts mentioned at the beginning of this section was passed in 1982, it brought about the demise of borstal institutions, at one time the glory of the English penal system.

It is ironic that though, in the spirit of the May Report recommendations, a massive programme of building new prisons and refurbishing old ones was announced in 1983, two years later the prison population touched an all-time high of over 48,000,[25] a figure that it was anticipated would not be reached until the 1990s. And, as I write these lines, I have beside me the 1984 report of Her Majesty's Inspector of Prisons, which describes the Dickensian conditions still existing in many prisons: an 'unacceptable quality of life for the inmates', 'widespread idleness', financial and staffing constraints which are likely to 'gnaw at the fabric of many regimes for some time to come', and the probability 'that a significant proportion of the prison population will still be using chamber pots at the end of the century'. This distressing picture helps to explain why little has changed since, a decade ago, a highly respected commentator concluded that a 'penological pessimism' has replaced the 'penological optimism' which still informed our prisons and borstals at the end of the War and in the early years after.[26]

And yet that is not the whole picture. Even this brief account of penal history would be sadly misleading if it failed to pay tribute to the dedicated service and at times heroic perseverance of so many men and women who, despite enormous difficulties, have striven to improve conditions and to help those in their care. It is not simply from my reading but from personal experience during one brief period of that history that I can speak with confidence of members of staff at every level in the penal system who have been fired with a genuine desire to serve their fellow men and women in prison. In not a few cases their care and deep humanity have been motivated by the gospels and supported by personal prayer.

If, despite so much good will and so many efforts over the course of so many decades, prisons still fall so far short of what we might reasonably hope for, could that be because we have been attempting the impossible? Could it be that one of the oddest mistakes in history was the decision to erect monastery-like institutions, and cloister within them tens of thousands of human beings who have neither the calling, nor the inclination, nor in most cases the natural or spiritual resources, to derive any real benefit from a monastic way of life – without the option?

4

PRISON PARISH

The degree of civilisation in a society can by judged by entering its prisons.

(Fyodor Dostoevsky)

George Bernard Shaw once argued that 'The public conscience would be far more active if the punishment of imprisonment were abolished and we went back to the rack, the stake, the pillory, and the lash at the cart's tail ... It would be far better (for the offender) to suffer in the public eye; for among the crowd of sightseers there might be a Victor Hugo or a Dickens, able and willing to make the sightseers think of what they are doing ... The prisoner has no such chance ... the secrecy of the prison makes it hard to convince the public that he is suffering at all'.[1]

Like many another outrageous Shavian argument, this one is not without its element of truth. In recent times the Home Office has adopted a much more open policy towards the media. Newspaper articles and television series, such as Rex Bloomstein's *Strangeways* and the ever-popular *Porridge* with its satirical quality of simultaneously evoking laughter and delivering a message, have helped to make the public much more aware of what happens in prison. Yet for all that, prisoners and their concerns do not feature prominently in the minds of most people and prisons themselves remain essentially hidden, secret places – little, self-contained worlds with everything they need: workshops and exercise yards, classrooms and cinema, canteen (a shop selling tobacco, toothpaste, birthday cards, etc.) and hospital or sick bay, chapel and gymnasium, kitchen, barber's shop and library. Prisons are unique in functioning twenty-four hours a day for 365 days every year, yet never being able to put up a 'No Vacancies' sign at their front gate, or refuse to accept anyone whom the courts choose to send them.

Those of us who have a prison for our parish often find it difficult to convey to others what life 'inside' is really like. Part of the difficulty stems from the fact that penal institutions are so numerous and so varied; as the maps in Appendix B illustrate, they are dotted across England and Wales from Acklington near Amble in the far north to the Isle of Wight in the south, and from Blundeston in the east to Swansea in the west; even in Scotland and Northern Ireland, where, in absolute terms, they are far fewer, their number is still high, especially in Scotland, relative to the populations of the respective territories. Not only are prisons numerous throughout the United Kingdom, they also cater for different kinds of offenders: for men and women and young people; for those on remand, awaiting trial or sentence, and those already sentenced; for those who represent a serious threat to the community and those who are little more than social nuisances.

Furthermore, the institutions themselves fall into different types; in the adult sector, there is the two-fold division into local and training prisons. The latter are often modern, well-equipped and sited in rural localities; they usually allow inmates greater freedom and aim to provide them with better opportunities so far as education, work, physical education and other facilities are concerned. They cover a spectrum of institutions, from the dispersal prisons, mentioned in the last chapter, which incorporate sophisticated security features, to the open prisons which often have nothing more than a perimeter fence to mark their boundaries. In his own inimitable fashion, the governor of one open prison used to conclude his address to new arrivals with these words: 'You are here on trust. If any of you decides to clear off, please don't climb over the fence. You may well damage yourself. Worse still, you may damage my fence. So, leave in a civilised manner – by the main gate, after the day staff have gone off duty. We won't chase you, but in due course the police will pick you up and return you to a local prison'.

The implied threat in the final phrase was unmistakable: local prisons are generally regarded as the fag-end of the penal system. They are usually situated in cities; they are old, dating from the prison-building spree of over a hundred years ago; they are overcrowded, with few facilities; they fulfil such a multiplicity of tasks – servicing the courts, housing prisoners, classifying inmates and transferring them where appropriate to training prisons, etc. – that they have been described as the penal 'maids-of-all-work'.

However, despite the number and variety of penal institutions, and despite the boast one often hears from staff and prisoners, that 'There is no other Nick in the country like this one', I think we might justifiably take life in a local prison as a paradigm for imprisonment in general: first, because all prisoners spend some, and many of them all, of their sentence in local prisons, and, second, because at any time throughout the year it is in these prisons that almost 40 per cent of the total prison population is to be found. Furthermore, if the regime of, for example, a training prison or an open Youth Custody centre is far more civilised than that of a local prison, there is no form of imprisonment which does not carry with it some of the dangers and pains that are so apparent within the walls of a local institution.

A kind of dying

Over the past half-century a number of studies have tried to assess the effects of imprisonment upon those who endure it.[2] They have shown that prison is a complex community with a variety of pressures and influences at work, an 'informal' as well as a 'formal' organisation, and a powerful tendency to institutionalise all who belong to it. The American criminologist Gresham Sykes insists that: 'In attempting ... to understand the meaning of imprisonment ... we must see the prison as a society within a society'. It is what the modern sociologist would call a 'total institution', that is to say: 'A place of residence and work where a large number of like-situated individuals, cut off from the wider society for an appreciable period of time, together lead an enclosed, formally administered round of life'.[3] Prisoners, like small children, live and work and sleep and take their recreation under the same roof; unlike the rest of us, who after a disappointing day at work can go home and forget all about it, they have no means of escaping from the place where they experienced disappointments or misfortunes. Worse still, they tend to be regimented, to be treated alike; the system requires that they – like small children – do exactly what they are told, whatever their own personal feelings or difficulties.

It is hardly surprising, then, that a 'total institution' is said to have a 'mortifying' (literally, a 'killing') effect on its inmates; it tends to demean them, degrade them, rob them of self-esteem. It was a young prisoner, innocent of the jargon of the specialists, who expressed these ideas very perceptively in a letter he wrote to his chaplain. It ran as follows: 'Have you ever thought of some of the experiences which accompany ... death – some of the experiences which are the consequence of death? I ask you this surprising question ... because being a prisoner has made me parallel imprisonment and death. The initial, unpleasant experience of having to strip oneself naked in the prison reception room embodies all that follows within the prison environment. When we die, we can take nothing with us; everything material that we possess is left behind ... when we are imprisoned, we are no longer able to determine what we would like to wear, what things we would like to have around us, what we wish to eat, etc. etc. But these material concerns become insignificant in the face of having to relinquish the close relationship with our loved ones. It is rather like dying: we remain conscious of all that is happening to our nearest and dearest, but there is very little we can do about it. However great the problems or crisis, we are powerless to help or to succour; we can only depend on the goodness and charity of others'.

The 'dying', as that young man suggested, begins with what happens to a prisoner during the reception procedure – or perhaps even earlier as he passes through the prison gates – especially if he is a first-timer. With the thoughts of all that transpired in court still in mind, the accusations, the public and detailed revelation of his wrongdoing, the finding of guilt, followed maybe by the stinging rebuke of the judge or magistrate and then the passing of sentence – he is now stripped of his own clothing and all his possessions, bathed, medically examined, dressed in prison uniform of bluey-grey serge trousers, lapel-less jacket, blue and white striped shirt, unbreakable blue tie and grey socks, and then issued with a number: from now on he is 723401 Mortlake. He receives his cell kit: plastic knife (thoughtfully blunted), fork, spoon, mug and plate. Before long he will be photographed – left profile, right profile, full-face – and fingerprinted; and these 'mug shots' and 'tabs' will follow him wherever he goes: he has become a marked man.

I do not mean to suggest that there are not good practical reasons for the reception procedure, but simply ask you to consider what it may feel like to be on its receiving end. As one ex-prisoner explained, as he reflected on his own experience: 'The clothes I take off will be out of date when I come out, and as I watch a trusty gather them carelessly into his arms and disappear with them, I feel as if part of myself had been taken away'. Another prisoner reported: 'I've never been in jail before, it's like being plucked out of one world and dumped in another ... I survive by worrying about what's happening in this prison this week or next, and blotting out everything outside'.[4]

Naturally, different individuals react differently to their first taste of prison, but very many of them experience a whole range of emotions – fear, bewilderment, loneliness, shame, uncertainty, numbness, resignation – as they wait for the leisurely reception session to come to an end. But, finally, processed, kitted-out and numbered, they are taken by prison officers to the cell blocks. Their sentence proper has begun.

Come 'inside'

In the eighteenth century the Utilitarian philosopher Jeremy Bentham had envisaged the building of a national penitentiary, 'a mill', he described it, 'for grinding rogues honest and idle men industrious'. He called it the Panopticon (or 'All-seeing') because its circular structure and open planning would make it possible for a gaoler to see all that was happening throughout the institution; thus it had the 'fundamental advantage' of 'the *apparent* omnipresence of the inspector ... combined with the extreme facility of his *real presence*'.[5]

In fact the Panopticon never became a reality, but the principles behind it were incorporated into the penal establishments which sprang up in the Victorian era and continue today as local prisons. They each have a central hub, commonly referred to quite simply as 'the centre', with broad wings stretching out from it like the spokes of a wheel; each wing several storeys high, and each storey linked to the next by open iron staircases. Thus, in principle at any rate, an officer standing at the centre has a commanding view of all that is happening throughout the wings. The storeys consist of a flagged gallery, flanked on one side by the cells and looking out on the other to an open well covered with wire-netting to forestall any homicidal or suicidal attempts.

It is in this bleak, bizarre setting that prisoners will spend months or even years of their life 'inside'. Most of them seem to accept it philosophically enough most of the time. I have often been impressed, especially in male prisons, by the spirit of camaraderie and sense of humour, but I am too familiar with the scene to take it at its face value. Prisons, by and large, are dark, miserable places where there is almost always a great deal of suffering and unhappiness just beneath the surface. This is how one prisoner described his impressions of life 'inside': 'Prison for me means greyness, filth and a terrible sense of not being needed. The lack of ability to try and do something for oneself, and above all loneliness. One just gives up unless one is terribly strong. It's something that only a person who has served a sentence of imprisonment can understand'.[6]

Behind those words one can detect the sense of stigma that so many prisoners feel. If 'self is a social construct', what sort of self-image can a man have when he sees himself regarded by society as best removed from the scene? When he is stripped of so many of the things that might enable him to preserve a sense of worth and self-mastery – his own clothes, his possessions, the ability to order his own life and care for his own family? When work, if there is any at all, may last only two or three hours a day, and is probably dull and repetitive (even in 1986 there are still prisoners employed in sewing mail-bags)? And when wages, amounting to no more than a few pounds a week, are more likely to undermine than to enhance his human dignity?

Nor, unhappily, do the stigmatising effects of imprisonment come to an end when the sentence is completed. I once came across a wayside pulpit which bore the message: 'Have you paid for your sins?' and beneath it a wit had added: 'If you have, kindly ignore this notice'! But, as many a prisoner will say: 'It's not now, it's when you've gone through those gates, it's when you've paid for your crimes, that the real punishment begins'. And if that views seems unduly cynical, it is powerfully borne out by an acknowledged expert in the penological field, who writes: 'The greatest need for reform exists outside the prisons in the hearts and minds of the ordinary members of the community. Greater understanding of the problems faced by ex-prisoners is needed as well as better appreciation of our own need for scapegoats ... if half the energies which are devoted to the attack on the prisons could be directed towards the improvement in community attitudes and the promotion of more tolerance and understanding, there would be a much better prospect of prisoners' reform, which after all must be at least part of what it is all about'.[7]

Some men, especially the regulars, do not resent a spell 'inside' – 'a bit of a rest', they say, or even 'a break from the wife' – but many more are only too conscious of the dreadful waste of life that a prison sentence represents, the sheer futility of it all. It would be unjust to underestimate the immense efforts made by so many members of staff – teachers, P.E. instructors, probation officers, works officers, etc. – to help those in their charge, or to deny the benefits that some prisoners gain, in terms of educational achievements, physical fitness, job and social skills. Nonetheless, the majority of inmates seem to leave prisons with little, if anything, to show for their time 'inside'. Sadder than that, some are only too well aware that they have lost experiences that can never come their way again. It was while returning from prison one day that I heard on the radio A. E. Housman's poem in which he describes how as a young man he was filled with wonder at the beauty of the cherry tree in bloom, and continues:

> Now, of my threescore years and ten,
> Twenty will not come again,
> And take from seventy springs a score,
> It only leaves me fifty more.
>
> And since to look at things in bloom
> Fifty springs are little room,
> About the woodlands I will go,
> To see the cherry hung with snow.

But there are more precious experiences than the sight of a cherry tree in spring time. Housman's words gave particular poignancy to a conversation I had held with another young man only hours before, when he had told me amidst tears how bitterly he regretted the fact that he had missed for ever the experience of watching his little girl as she spoke her first words, took her first faltering steps and passed through the other stages of early childhood.

Of course, separation from families and friends constitutes perhaps the bitterest ingredient of imprisonment: there are scarcely any opportunities for a natural show of tender feelings or emotions. It was a wise old chaplain who once said to me: 'Have you realised that "inside" virtually the only physical contacts are made in the context of violence or homosexuality?' When a married prisoner begins a sentence, the prisoner and the spouse are put into a kind of emotional cold-storage. They have no means of expressing their deepest feelings for each other, apart from their weekly letter and their half-hour monthly visit.[8] But letters are normally censored: it is not easy to reveal your heart to a loved one by means of a letter which is to be read by someone else. And during visits the couple are separated by the width of a table, with many other couples – as well as countless children – sharing the same meeting place, and prison officers always hovering in the background; it is not easy to converse with a loved one, when time is short and there are distractions on every side and the visit must end, at someone else's bidding, with a hurried, public embrace. Little wonder, that letters and visits, though ardently looked forward to, often leave the recipients more distressed than they were before. A chance remark in conversation, an obscure sentence in a letter can be rehearsed in the imagination time and again, and interpreted in the most pessimistic way. There is a constant fear that a spouse will be unfaithful or even desert the prisoner; and, on the part of long-term male prisoners especially, additional fear about their sexual potency.

There is a further element of imprisonment that might easily be overlooked, and that is the forced association with other criminals. It is an element which the House of Commons Expenditure Committee considered it important to highlight: 'To lose the freedom of movement and association, to lose effectively any choice over food, place of work, choice of one's friends, and the company of one's family – these are amongst some of the real deprivations of prison today. But that is not all. The true harshness of prison life does not stem solely from the deprivation of liberty and limited choice, nor from the actual physical conditions, but from the daily or hourly pressures which prisoners inflict on each other. One must recognise the element of personal insecurity involved in a situation, where the weakest are exposed to the strongest, the vilest and most violent, where the more powerful dominate and constantly intimidate'.[9] Nor, as we shall see, is there necessarily any escape from the 'company' even in one's cell.

The door that says it all

Some time ago the French newspaper *La Croix* carried a novel article entitled 'Doors'.[10] Its author, an urban architect, described the shape and size and texture and mechanisms of almost every kind of door you could imagine. There was, however, one exception. Perhaps you could not expect an architect to have much to say about a cell door – unless of course he had known what it was like to be on the wrong side of one. Nonetheless, several of his remarks, sometimes in a paradoxical way, had me pondering on that heavy, metal-clad door which marks the entrance of a prison cell.

> To go through a door is to alter your condition ... you become a patient, a client, a passenger ...

Apart from the door of death itself, it is hard to think of any door which so transforms the condition of the one who passes through it as does the door of a prison cell. It is the last frontier between freedom and captivity; to cross this threshold is finally to become a prisoner, not only confined *to* a penal institution but confined *within* it. For the duration of the sentence, this cell will be home: a prisoner will spend more time here than in any other part of the prison. Indeed, unless he or she has a job to go to – and many in local prisons have not – the inmate may be 'banged up' for twenty-three hours out of twenty-four, with just two thirty-minute periods of exercise each day, which consists of walking round and round the concentric paths of the prison yard.

The cell itself is approximately eleven feet long, seven feet wide and nine feet high; 'it's like living in a bathroom', as one governor put it.[11] Its furniture consists of a bed, a chair and table, an open cabinet, cutlery, a bowl and soap dish, a shaving brush and razor, a toothbrush and toothpaste, a hairbrush or comb, a mug, a board for photographs of family and friends, though more often covered with pin-ups, a 60-watt bulb and a chamber pot. This list indicates that the cell is not only bedroom, but sitting-room, dining-room and, during the hours of night, toilet also.

To open a door and go inside is to behave in a way appropriate to the place you have entered – boss's office, restaurant, motor car, church …

The one hope you might entertain for prisoners is that they will not become too conditioned to the behaviour appropriate to a cell. An officer I was speaking to shortly after I became a chaplain, nodded in the direction of an inmate and remarked: 'You can be sure that fellow will return here'. He must have noticed my puzzled expression, for he added by way of explanation: 'Just look at his shoes: you can see your face in them. He's a model prisoner, and, you'll find out, model prisoners always come back'. I still am not convinced of the validity of the shoe-shine test, but I understand now what the officer was getting at: prisoners can easily become conformist, settle down to prison life and what is expected of them, and they are then well on the way to being institutionalised.

To lock men and women for long hours within the confines of a cell, where they follow an utterly predictable daily routine, with no decisions to make and little to do except read and listen to the radio and talk with cell-mates, is hardly calculated to bring the best out of them. If it changes them at all, the likelihood is that it will be for the worse. The allegation is sometimes made that prison is too soft, and in a sense that is true, but as a former Director of the Howard League for Penal Reform has written: 'The softness which really merits criticism is the removal (from prisoners) of all responsibility'.[12] It was the night before he was due to return to his wife and three children that I went to visit one of my friends. 'I bet you can hardly wait for tomorrow', I said enthusiastically, 'it must feel great.' Surprisingly, he replied, with rather less enthusiasm: 'Yes, I'll be glad to get home, but you know, in another way I'm not too sure. You don't have any responsibilities here, nothing much to worry about, really; it's when you go through those gates that the trouble begins'. Like many of his comrades that man was the victim of the really damaging 'softness' of prison life.

To open a door is to welcome someone in, invite him to share your home ... To close a door is to guard against intruders – even if they are only the cold or the draught – it is to assert ownership.

Prisoners, however, unless they happen to be in one of the modern prisons, do not have the key to their own front door; they are in no position to open it: for that, they must depend upon others. Just as they cannot open the door, so they cannot keep it closed at will. The writings of Konrad Lorenz, which describe how savagely animals react to the invasion of their 'space', throw some light on why prisoners resent the cell-searches that have to be made, especially if they are carried out in an insensitive or provocative way. Still more of course do they resent body searches, which are usually no more than a 'rub down' (a swift movement of an officer's hand over their clothing), but in some cases takes the form of a 'strip search' (involving the removal of clothing).

As for the door keeping out the cold and draughts, I have been in cells so oppressive in the summer months that the 'owners' broke the small panes of glass, which make up the window, to let the fresh air circulate more freely, and a few months later stuffed the same windows with socks and underpants to keep out the winter cold!

The heat was not due entirely to the summer weather. It was due also to overcrowding: some seven thousand cells, designed originally for one, now hold two or even three prisoners, together with a doubling or trebling of the furnishings. It was in an attempt to convey to its readers what life can be like under such conditions that the first annual report of H.M. Inspector of Prisons carried the following paragraph: 'If any reader unfamiliar with the prison system finds it difficult to picture the squalor in which many inmates of local prisons are expected to spend their sentence, let him imagine finding himself obliged to stay in an hotel so overbooked that he has to share his room with two complete strangers. The room itself is so cramped that there is little space for his clothes or personal possessions, and if he wants to walk up and down, the other occupants must first lie on their beds. Worse, the hotel management insists that guests remain in their rooms for all but an hour or so a day and must take their meals there. As a result the atmosphere rapidly becomes fetid, especially since neither the reader nor his room mates have been able to take a bath for some days. But not only is there no basin or bath available, there is no lavatory either, and the reader and his companions are faced with the prospect of relying for the foreseeable future upon chamber pots thoughtfully provided by the management. If the reader does not conclude that such an experience lasting several days would be degrading and brutalising, he is being less than honest with himself: how much worse would it be after several weeks?'[13]

The door of our room guarantees our privacy ...

But, then, there is no judas-hole fitted into the doors of our homes. In prison, cell doors give no assurance of privacy, not even to inmates who are on their own: for at any hour of day or night an eye may be peering through the opened peep-hole, the inmates, whatever they happen to be doing, may be under surveillance. A modern-day Cain must not be able to escape from view! Like so many other features of prison life, the judas-hole can easily be justified; it is often a safeguard for the inmates. But I cannot be alone in experiencing a feeling of sadness that there are fellow human beings who because of their misdeeds have forfeited their right not only to liberty but to privacy, too.

Easing the pain

Given that prison is 'a society within a society', and a 'total' society at that, it is hardly unexpected that its inmates share a sub-culture of their own. There is a scholarly view that this sub-culture is nothing other than a direct importation of the criminal sub-culture from outside. While prisoners do undoubtedly bring with them the values and standards of home, it is difficult to disagree with Gresham Sykes' claim that the inmate code is primarily a response to prison conditions and a means of easing what he calls 'the pains of imprisonment'.

'As a population of prisoners moves in the direction of solidarity, as demanded by the inmate sub-culture, the pains of imprisonment become less severe...' he argues. 'A cohesive inmate society provides the prisoner with a meaningful social group with which he can identify himself and which will support him in his struggle against his condemners.'[14] This quotation indicates only too clearly that the inmate social system centres around 'us' and 'them': having been rejected, prisoners in their turn reject their rejectors, who are epitomised by the prison staff. And so, the story goes, 'Cons always stick together' and 'All screws are bastards'. Of course, neither statement is accurate, but each serves as a rallying cry. In fact, the solidarity existing among prisoners is often flimsier than it looks, easily disintegrating under the weight of divergent interests and ambitions; and the prison staff, while they themselves would be the last to suggest that they are beyond criticism, sometimes gain the respect, and even the admiration, of the inmates. For all that, however, the 'us' and 'them' division is real enough in the prison world.

There are other tendencies which are encouraged by the prison sub-culture. First, the tendency of inmates to underestimate themselves, to have a low opinion of themselves. A group of young prisoners was asked how they would feel if the three monks, who were due to conduct a mission in the institution, were to share their life with them so far as they could: they would eat with the inmates, join them in their recreation, sleep in the cells, and so on. The response of the youngsters showed that they were bewildered at the idea that anyone in his right mind 'would freely choose to come down to our level'. It is not difficult to see how those who feel that they are inferior to other human beings will often be tempted to argue: 'They say we're good-for-nothing, let's really be good for nothing'.

Not unrelated to this is the tendency of prisoners to glamorise crime, their own and others'. Every cat burglar is really a 'great train robber', if you take him at his word: he wants to impress, to show that he is a hard man. Jimmy Boyle's long personal experience of prison led him to the conclusion that it is 'all part of the sub-culture for everyone to go about trying to impress everyone else. The fact is that prison eats your insides out. All of this takes place when you are alone, but it wouldn't be the done thing to let this be seen by other people'.[15]

I once came across a perfect example of this need to preserve the macho image, at all costs, before one's peers. It was the day after three police detectives were shot down in cold blood outside Wormwood Scrubs: I found myself talking to a knot of prisoners who had gathered in one of the cells. They were discussing with some relish the events of the night before and expressing delight that 'another three bastards' had got what they deserved. I tried in vain to bring them to a different frame of mind. Gradually, they disappeared, one after another, until eventually only one prisoner and myself were left in the cell. He looked up at me from the bed where he was sitting: 'You know', he began, 'I don't really agree with them. I feel sick for those coppers and their wives and families. I told the other lads that, but, well, you know, they all ganged up on me, and you can't be the odd man out in a place like this, can you?'

There is another tendency, which is the antithesis of the one just described: prisoners sometimes cannot bring themselves to admit their culpability. Understandably defensive, they will constantly protest their innocence or complain about the severity of their punishment. In some cases, if they owned up to their crimes or allowed themselves to be too acutely aware of the terrible evils they have done, they might be tempted to commit suicide or risk reprisals from their fellows.

Unhappily, one of the characteristic tendencies of prisoners is to make scapegoats of certain types of criminals, especially those guilty of sex offences and in particular offences involving youngsters. Perhaps it is an attempt on the part of the victimisers to ease their own sense of guilt: when you are at the bottom of the pile, it is good to find someone else who can take your place; it is a relief to be able to say: 'Well, I may have done wrong, but at least I wouldn't descend to the depths that fellow did'. One of the prison rules, number 43, expressly arranges for prisoners to be placed in a special wing in solitary confinement, or at any rate with others who have committed similar offences, for their 'own protection· These 'rule 43s' are one of the saddest sights in the penal system – not simply men and women who have been rejected by society, but men and women who have been rejected by their fellow prisoners: the outcasts of the outcasts. It was a Member of Parliament, addressing a Chaplains' Conference shortly after his first visit to a rule 43 wing, who told us: 'As I walked through that wing and talked to the men I recalled the story of Zacchaeus, and I couldn't but believe that if our Lord were to pay a visit to one of our prisons, he would make a bee-line for the rule 43s'.

A further tendency that the prison sub-culture encourages is that of fantasising and exaggerating. Fantasising, because when men and women have little mental stimulation, they may compensate by allowing their imagination to run riot or by retreating into themselves and the universe of their own making which is outside institutional control. Exaggerating, because when the shrunken little world of prison is, for the time being, an inmate's only world, everything looms large; things that would be of little consequence outside, suddenly assume momentous proportions. An ounce of 'weed' (tobacco) is regarded as a treasure: a woman who has recently written of her experience of imprisonment recalls that ' ... all the serious trouble I saw ... was caused by tobacco, or rather the lack of it'.[16] A delay over mealtimes – when there is a firmly controlled programme of rising, 'slopping out', work, meals, lights out – is an extraordinary upsetting of the day; an expected letter which does not materialise is a minor tragedy. It is noticeable among older prisoners how they have an eye for detail 'inside' and give it significance, even to the detriment of thinking and planning for their future. For them life is now, and the world is here.

Finally, there is the tendency for a first-rate 'grapevine' to emerge. Prisoners have time on their hands; time to observe, to note, to interpret; time to pay attention to the sound of footsteps, the inflection of voices outside the cell; time, and a strong desire at times, to ferret out information about the prison system and those who work in it. And this information is quickly shared with their peers. About two months before my predecessor retired, I stopped to talk to a group of men who were sitting out in the sun – at that time I was chaplain to an open prison – when one of them stunned me with the announcement: 'I believe you're in line for promotion; you'll be going to London soon; did you know?' I did not know, nor, I suspect, did anyone else. Presumably, it was all shrewd guesswork, but it left me with a high regard for prisoners' ability to gather and interpret and share information.

Throughout this section I have repeatedly referred to 'tendencies'. Though the presence of a sub-culture with all its strange dynamics may be inevitable in the prison setting, there is no inevitability about the effect it will have on the individual prisoner. At best, the social controls of the inmate community are only partially effective. Many will violate the 'code', whenever it suits their interests; some seem able to withstand it completely. Shortness of sentence, lack of integration with the prisoner group, maintenance of good relationships with family, taking advantage of educational programmes – all these help to reduce the danger of institutionalisation. They lessen the risk that prison will serve as an advanced course in crime rather than as a help and encouragement to the leading of 'a good and useful life'.[17]

Some holiday camp!

As long ago as the 1820s complaints were being heard that transportation should be stopped, because it let the criminal off too lightly, encouraged rather than deterred the would-be wrong-doer and contradicted the principle of 'less eligibility'.[18] In the original context of the Poor Law, this principle meant that the conditions enjoyed by paupers should be 'less eligible' than those enjoyed by 'the lowest grade of independent labourer'. In the context of punishment, it means that prisoners should not fare as well as, indeed if anything should fare rather less well than, law-abiding citizens. Today that same principle is frequently resurrected, usually in a very emotive guise. Why, we are asked, should young thugs be housed in holiday camps? Why should elderly and defenceless old women who have been mugged live in worse conditions than their muggers?

Natually, it is lamentable that anyone should live in inhuman conditions. The fact that some do, including some who are the victims of crime, does not justify us in deliberately imposing such conditions on others, even on criminals. As I indicated earlier, one of the basic principles of penal policy in modern times has been that imprisonment is itself the punishment for crime; there can be no justification for deliberately adding to that punishment. The 'holiday camp' argument is particularly feeble: how many jolly holiday campers would stomach being locked in at night, forbidden the company of the opposite sex, allowed scarcely any choices, provided with little entertainment, and compelled to queue up each morning to empty their chamber pots down a common sluice? Yet, that is how many prisoners have to live.

There is, of course, a growing number of new, well-appointed prisons. Even these aim to provide not luxury, but conditions that befit the dignity of human beings according to twentieth-century standards, not those of a hundred years ago. As a humane society we can hardly be content with less. And if, at times, the cries for harsher, more punitive conditions in prison grow louder it is useful to reflect on the old proverb: 'No man loveth his fetters, be they made of gold'.[19]

In July 1980 a seminar was held under the auspices of the Council of Europe at Bagshot Park, Surrey. Its theme was: 'The Chaplaincy contribution to Penal Thought and Practice', and it was attended by prison chaplains of all the major Christian denominations from all over Europe. One of the speakers was Bishop Augustine Harris who had himself been a prison chaplain in England for a dozen years. In the opening paragraph of what proved to be a thought-provoking paper on

'The Penal System – A Theological Assessment', he boldly declared: 'God doesn't like prisons. God doesn't like penal systems'.[20] There was no word of protest from anyone; instead, that almost tangible deepening of silence that indicates that a speaker has struck a responding chord in his audience.

We agreed with what the bishop was saying. Agreed with him, not because he happened to be a bishop, but because he spoke from experience; like his listeners, he knew at first hand what it means to have a prison as your parish.

5

PRISON PARISHIONERS

The police seek in every human being a murderer;
the wise man and the philosopher seek in every murderer a human being.
We Christians seek God in every person ... even in murderers.
And each of us will find what he seeks:
the police will find their murderer;
the philosophers will find their human beings;
and we, we shall find God in every person.

(Virgil Georghiu)[1]

I had just given a talk in which, among other things, I had outlined some of the damaging effects that often result from imprisonment. It had come to question time, and the first person to his feet was asking pointedly: 'If things "inside" really are as bad as the speaker makes out, I wonder why he doesn't do the honourable thing and resign from the Prison Service Chaplaincy?'

A similar question might have been posed to Bishop Harris when he addressed that European gathering of chaplains described at the end of the last chapter: if God doesn't like prisons, as he alleged, why had he stayed on as a prison chaplain for more than a decade? It is not for me to suggest how the bishop might have defended himself. But what I can say is that my response to the questioner who had put me on the spot began with some other words of the bishop, in fact the words immediately following upon those already reported. God may not like prisons and prison systems, 'but God does love everybody in the prison system'.[2]

Those of us who have a prison for our parish are buoyed up by the certain knowledge that all our parishioners – whether prisoners or prison staff or their respective families – are loved by God. And if God loves them, it is simply inconceivable that we should abandon them, however grim the circumstances in which they find themselves, and whatever we may think about penal systems.

Prisoners are people

Among my prized possessions is a mascot about eighteen inches tall: it is
in the form of a monkey, clad in Everton strip – which is only right when
its owner is an Everton supporter – holding a banana in one hand and a
football rattle in the other. It was a gift, made for me by a man who knew
my sporting proclivities, a man who used to spend most of his free time
making soft toys for handicapped children and transcribing books into
braille for the blind. It is many years since we last met, but at that time he
was serving his twenty-first prison sentence. His handiwork has served a
purpose which I am sure he never had in mind: it has been a constant
reminder to me that, before anything else, prisoners are people. People
like you and me. People who offer gifts to their friends. People with
hopes and fears and ambitions and longings. People who are not wholly
good, but not wholly bad either – just like the rest of us. With Shylock
they can argue: 'Hath not a (prisoner) eyes? hath not (a prisoner) hands,
organs, dimensions, senses, affections, passions? fed with the same food,
hurt with the same weapons, healed by the same means, warmed and
cooled by the same winter and summer'[3] as the rest of the human race?

I have to confess that before I became a prison chaplain, I was quite
content to regard men and women 'inside' quite simply as criminals
getting what they deserved. Not only did I fail to appreciate that they are
a very mixed bag indeed – how can petty thieves and cold-blooded
murderers be lumped together simply as criminals? – or that some of
them at least were less deserving of punishment than their situation
might suggest; but worse still, I failed to recognise that there is so much
more to be said about prisoners than the fact that they have fallen foul of
the law.

It was an inmate who shrewdly observed that 'prison is a place where
one discovers how good people are and how bad people can be'.[4] The
badness is, in a sense, what we might expect, the same dreary badness –
violence, greed, ingratitude, untruthfulness and so on – that is to be
found on every side in the world outside, and within ourselves. But the
goodness shines through, too, in all kinds of ways, and it is the more
welcome because it appears in such an improbable setting. So many
people who have had the opportunity of working with prisoners readily
admit that they seem to have gained at least as much as they have given.
They speak of prisoners' patience, their tolerance, their unexpected
honesty, their extraordinary kindness to each other, and, perhaps as a
direct result of their experience of imprisonment, their concern for those
who are 'imprisoned' by handicaps or sickness or poverty.

There is an almost unending catalogue of prisoners' 'good deeds' that
might be recorded: a group of young offenders who constructed a special
therapeutic swimming bath for paraplegic youngsters; some prisoners at
Channings Wood who, inspired by Bob Geldof's 'Live Aid' concert, got
permission to run their own concert in the prison, to which outsiders

could be invited, and raised over £1,500 for Ethiopian relief; a band of boys from an open borstal who worked in a home for mentally and physically handicapped and who, according to the superintendent, showed far more sensitivity and understanding in dealing with the invalids than did the group of boys from a public school who had worked there before; the prisoners who collected from their own meagre resources for eleven different charities and threw a Christmas party in the prison recreation room for senior citizens of the locality.

Because of the constraints of their situation, the goodness of prisoners often expresses itself in small ways, which might easily go unnoticed, but is none the less important for that. An experienced chaplain recalls how, after a serious disturbance in a dispersal prison, all the lifers were locked in their cells for twenty-three hours a day. They were only opened up, six at a time, for feeding and 'slopping out'. The chaplains were busy getting round to visit them. In one cell was Joe, serving a life sentence with a recommended twenty-five years' minimum for a brutal murder. He could neither read nor write but he used to spend hours tuned in to his radio. 'I heard a good programme last night', he announced, 'and the speaker – I think he was a parson – said it is better to give than receive. Do you know, he's right? When I was "slopping out", the guy in the next cell told me his radio battery was flat, so I decided to give him mine. It was then I realised how right it is that it's better to give than to take.' At first hearing, there might seem to be nothing very remarkable in the incident, but when you remember that this man – this 'murderer', you recall – was illiterate, was spending twenty-three hours per day cooped up alone in his cell, and had no chance of getting replacements for the batteries until after the weekend – it was now Saturday morning – then, his little act of kindness was not perhaps so little, after all.

A similar experience occurred when I was celebrating Mass in Holloway prison. It was a summer's day, but the central heating, with a perversity I have come across in other institutions, stubbornly refused to be switched off. I could feel the beads of perspiration running down my back and dripping off the end of my nose. Suddenly, out of the corner of my eye, I saw one of the women stepping forward towards the altar, holding something white in her hand. For a moment I wondered what was about to happen; then, I realised that she was offering me a paper handkerchief. I took it gratefully and, after carefully wiping my brow, slipped it into my pocket, in readiness for the next mopping-up operation, and promptly forgot all about the incident. A few days later I received a short note from an 'outsider' who had been present at the service. She said how much she had enjoyed being there, and, in particular, how touched she had been by 'the girl with the paper hanky'. 'As I saw it happening', she wrote, 'the thought that came to my mind was how Jesus noticed and responded to the widow woman who gave all she had.' Reading the note, I realised that the kindness of the prisoner woman, so ready to stretch out and share one of her few possessions with me, would not have gone unnoticed by the Lord – even if it had been quickly forgotten by her perspiring brother.

A governor, who was invited to give a lecture to a group of new chaplains, tried to help them to get things into perspective from the start. 'If I were to fit you chaps out in prison uniform', he told them, 'and put you in a cell in my prison, I very much doubt if anyone would notice any real difference between you and the rest of the cons – except of course for the way you speak!' I wonder, however, if the governor was not being a little too generous: there are articulate prisoners who would put many a cleric to shame.

During the papal visit in 1982 a chaplain from Wetherby borstal (as it then was) took some of the lads to York racecourse to see the Pope. They were all rigged out in ordinary clothes and the chaplain, too, decided to wear 'civvies' so that he would not attract undue attention to his little group. Shortly after their arrival, they got into conversation with a middle-aged lady who was obviously impressed by their conversation and behaviour.

Suddenly one of the borstal lads pointed towards the chaplain: 'You wouldn't guess he was a priest, would you?' he asked her. 'Well, I don't know', replied the good lady, obviously a bit taken aback. 'I think perhaps I might. But what about you lads, where are you all from?' The chaplain opened his mouth, but no words came. What could he say in this situation? He need not have worried; without a moment's hesitation one of the borstal boys was ready with a perfect reply: 'As a matter of fact, we're from a public school in Wetherby'. 'Are you really?', said the woman, 'I might have guessed as much.'

In so many ways a chaplain is reminded that his prison parishioners, despite their garb, are so much more than criminals. They are like the people next door or those over the road – or the chaplain himself. They are people of flesh and blood, each of them unique in his way and each of them loved by God.

Prisoners in close-up

Prisoners, like other people, are individuals, no two of them exactly alike. And yet there is a sense in which they do appear to have certain characteristics in common. I am not suggesting that all prisoners have all these characteristics, I am not even suggesting that every single prisoner has any one of them. I simply suggest that, after meeting thousands of prisoners over the course of many years, you find yourself building up a kind of identikit picture of what a prisoner is like. So, with the reminder that identikit pictures like passport photographs can be wildly misleading, let me introduce you to my 'Mr Average Prisoner'.

To begin with, my Mr Average Prisoner is not very bright. He may not be able to read and write – a report in 1980 estimated that some 18 per cent of inmates had a reading age of ten or less.[5] He may have picked up strange ideas which lead him to astonishing conclusions. I knew Graham well, and I knew he had to be taken seriously when he popped into the Question Box, whose contents I dealt with on the first Sunday of each month, the following query: 'I'd like to know, when I get out I am thinking of marrying my girl friend. But she has two babies, so I wonder if I could get married in hippy gear, and does my girl have to wear something pink to show she isn't a virgin? Could she wear a hippy mini-dress with pink flowers on it? or could she just put a pink flower wherever she wants to?' I recognised that this was not a question for public discussion, and so I had a long conversation with Graham in his cell. I think I managed to set his mind at rest, but I never did discover where the pink flower idea came from!

Prison education officers have helped prisoners to attain considerable academic successes, even at the level of the Open University, but perhaps their most undervalued work has been in the realm of remedial education. When a man who came into prison illiterate or semi-literate is able to return home with the newly acquired skill of coping with a tabloid newspaper or sharing a comic with his children, that must count as a considerable achievement, by any reckoning.

In the second place, my Mr Average Prisoner is addicted to drink or gambling, and, increasingly these days, to drugs and glue-sniffing. Much valuable work is done in prisons by groups like Alcoholics Anonymous and Gamblers Anonymous, but of course imprisonment itself is no remedy for addictions. The gambler still has endless opportunities for a flutter, though the currency may be nothing more than tobacco and the object of his bets rather less noble than the horses. Without an unacceptable degree of harassment it is impossible to prevent some drugs from slipping 'inside' from time to time. And while the man with a drink problem may not be able to put his fist round a glass of his favourite ale, he may well manage – usually in conjunction with some of his friends – to concoct a brew of his own. It was only after a painstaking search that the officers of one of the great local prisons finally located the supply of 'hooch' which they knew was lying around: they found it in a fire-extinguisher which had been emptied of its original contents, refilled with a prison-made brew and then replaced on the wall – an 'innocent' object which hardly deserved a second look.

Thirdly, my Mr Average Prisoner is emotionally immature: despite his physical development, he is a little boy who has never grown up. 'I could throttle some (of these prisoners)', said a prison officer on television, 'they're like children in men's bodies.'[6] And a consultant psychiatrist was making the same point when he wrote: 'there are areas of some prisons which resemble a toddler's play-pen within an adult orphanage'.[7] However, it must never be forgotten that prison, as was mentioned in the last chapter, itself tends to reinforce infantile behaviour. Children of all ages can be difficult – self-centred, quarrelsome, demanding, given to sulking and sometimes to tantrums, unable to see beyond the present moment – but when they are 'in men's bodies' the difficulties are compounded. The quarrels can erupt into violence, the tantrums take the form of 'breaking-up' everything in their cell that is destructible, the sulking develop into bouts of depression, the self-centredness lead to unreasonable demands upon members of staff.

In the course of many meetings with prisoners, I have come to notice two intriguing little features: the first is the amount of tattooing, though it is perhaps not quite so common nowadays as it was a decade or so ago, and the second is the manner of their handshakes, at least when they meet you for the first time. There appear to be more tattoos per square inch of prisoner flesh than you are likely to find anywhere else: sometimes they take the form of the letters L-O-V-E and H-A-T-E on the four fingers of each hand, sometimes the name of a girl friend – or the names of several successive girl friends – on their arms or chests, sometimes an elaborate design on their faces. As I sat with a young prisoner I found it impossible to prevent my eyes from following the course of the two snakes that were tattooed across his face: they inched several times round his ears, went down behind his neck and where their tails came to an end there was a dotted line, stretching across his throat, with the unnerving invitation 'Please cut here'.

As for the handshakes, they often come in one of two kinds: either the 'iron bar' variety – a stiff, unyielding hand as rigid as a piece of metal – or the 'dead fish' variety – a soft, clammy hand that seems to have no life of its own. In either case a marked contrast with the warm confident handshake that one is accustomed to receive. Could it be that this war-painting with tattoos and this distrustful handshaking reflect the underlying immaturity, or are a way of coping with the dismal self-image so common among prisoners? It was a wise and very compassionate psychiatrist in a youth custody centre who would regularly say to the youngsters who came to see her: 'Look, here's a piece of paper. Now you go away and don't come back until you have written down ten *good* things about yourself'.

Fourthly, my Mr Average Prisoner is longing for love and yet finds it hard to form lasting relationships, because he is the product of a broken home (broken, that is, by desertion, separation or divorce); or a home where parental discipline was unpredictable, veering from laxity to extreme harshness; or a home where there was little or no parental supervision. It is a governor of twenty-seven years' experience who wrote: 'Over ninety per cent of those in prison in this country today almost certainly come from broken homes'.[8] Behind that grim figure lie stories of neglect, cruel treatment, rejection, lack of love.

Take the case of Louis who revealed to his borstal housemaster that when his father died his mother had told him that he, still a lad in his teens, must now fill his father's role, ultimately to the extent of sharing her bed. The result, not surprisingly, was a dreadfully guilty and deeply wounded young man, who had carried his awful secret alone for many years. And there was Jimmy whose governor was reluctantly compelled to put him in solitary confinement over Christmastide for persistent bad behaviour. Later the lad remarked: 'Thanks, sir: that's the best Christmas I've ever had'. He was not trying to be clever; he was deadly serious. What a commentary on the childhood he had known that he was unable to recall a happier Christmas than the one he had spent alone in his cell.

On a lighter note, though this story too has its distressing side, a devoted borstal chaplain, gifted with a sense of humour, told me how a few days earlier he had met a new arrival whose two brothers, sister, father and mother were all doing time. 'I could just imagine the old man on his death-bed', the chaplain commented, 'I could see him musing to himself: "Well, my two lads are not doing too badly, one in borstal and the other in a detention centre; my girl's become a 'red-band' (a trusty), and the wife's got a cushy little number for herself in Holloway. All things considered, I haven't done too badly: 'Lord, now lettest thou thy servant depart in peace'!"'

A fifth characteristic of my Mr Average Prisoner is that he is more likely to have had psychiatric treatment than are people in the general population. There is no agreement about the precise number of prisoners who are suffering from mental disorder in terms of the Mental Health Act 1983, but it certainly runs to two or three hundred and perhaps many more. Because of the policy of greater openness in mental hospitals, consultants and nurses are loath to accept anti-social or disruptive patients. Furthermore, many inadequates with a history of mental illness or personality disorder, who formerly would have been placed in hospitals, now drift into prisons because of minor offences.

I will always remeber Alex. He was notorious for his violent behaviour – I have seen him go white with rage because, as he thought, another man touched his radio while he was trying to listen to the racing results. He began a sentence of six months but ended up doing a couple of years after several attacks on staff. Some years later, a friend of his told me that shortly after his release Alex had taken ill and finally died. A post-mortem revealed that he had two massive brain tumours. They had been there for many years. 'The marvel', commented the surgeon, 'is that he survived so long.' But there was another marvel, too: the Jekyll and Hyde behaviour of Alex now began to make sense: he was not simply 'a thoroughly bad lot'; he was a man who had had to tussle both with the temptations common to the human race and also with physical abnormalities which perhaps made him more victim than culprit.

Sixthly, my Mr Average Prisoner is young and unemployed, and may be homeless too. Crime is primarily a young man's game: perhaps 50 per cent of our prison population is made up of under-twenty-fives. A High Court Judge is reported to have said: 'I know of only two things which really dissuade people from crime: the first is age: they can no longer run faster than the police; and the second is some kind of conversion experience'. Unhappily she did not elaborate on what she meant by the latter, but some young men are dissuaded from crime by a religious conversion, many more by the experience of marriage, and others by finding a steady job. On a recent visit to a prison I passed through the kitchen area, where there was a group of fine, strapping young fellows, most of whom seemed to tower above the officer who was in charge. 'Do they give you much trouble?' I enquired. 'No, never', was his answer. Then he corrected himself: 'No trouble over discipline, anyway: the only difficulty is getting them to work. Most of that bunch have never had a job since they left school'.

In the seventh place, my Mr Average Prisoner is not a churchgoer: seldom more than a handful of the men I meet would describe themselves as anything more than nominal Christians. These were among the findings of a survey, conducted by the chaplain of a Youth Custody centre in 1985: most of the young men had minimal contact with the Church outside; almost a third had not been baptised and, incredibly, almost two-thirds said that their parents had never talked to them about religion. On the other hand a fair number said some prayers and came to chapel. Although only 40 per cent admitted any real belief in God, over twice that number accepted Jesus Christ as at least 'a good man' and, rather poignantly in the circumstances, those who believed in hell outnumbered those who believed in heaven![9]

However, such findings need to be interpreted with great care. Among prisoners, there is so much more goodness, so much more faith and so much more yearning for the Good News than might be imagined. It is unfair to judge them by ordinary standards of morality; the Lord expects them to act only in accordance with the light they have, and in some cases that light is little more than a fitful glimmer. Some of them see no incongruity in assaulting a child-molester while at the same time contributing to a collection for the child he assaulted, or having a crucifix or rosary beads hanging on the cell wall, side by side with the middle-page-spread of a glossy pornographic magazine.

An American friend of mine loves to tell how a couple came home one night to discover that though their home had been broken into, nothing seemed to have been taken. Then they found a note lying on the table which read: 'I broke into your house, intending to burgle it, but when I saw in the bedroom that picture of the mother with the baby Jesus on her knee, it reminded me of the picture we had at home. And so I decided not to steal anything, after all. Signed: Your Friend. P.S. I have taken the picture'. His behaviour may not have matched up to Christian standards in all respects – I wonder how often anyone's does? – but that young man had made progress, and as he slipped out of the house, the picture tucked under his coat, I like to believe that the Lord himself was smiling on him with approval.

Finally, my Mr Average Prisoner *is* a Mister: male prisoners outnumber female by a ratio of almost thirty to one; that is why they figure so prominently in these pages. But women must not be forgotten: in comparison with men, they are more likely to receive a custodial sentence for a first offence, and, according to some writers,[10] receive heftier sentences than do men found guilty of similar offences; an undue proportion of them seem to suffer from mental disorders; by and large, they find the restrictions of prison, especially the enforced separation from family, more painful than do their male counterparts; because female prisons and remand centres are so few in number – ten in England and Wales, and only one each in Scotland and Northern Ireland – women are often located far away from their own homes and their imprisonment can have devastating effects on their children.

For a variety of reasons then, the female inmate is an even sorrier spectacle than Mr Average Prisoner, and it is easy to sympathise with those who maintain that prison is no place for women and girls, in any but the most exceptional circumstances.

The 'invisible' victims

When a man (or woman) goes to prison the results might be compared to what happens when a stone, flung up by a passing car, crashes into your windscreen. It does not simply drill a neat hole at the point of impact: it shatters all the 'innocent' glass round about it. Similarly, imprisonment has harsh consequences not only for the prisoner, but for many other innocent people besides: it leaves behind a web of damage as its shattering effects reach out to family and friends, 'the invisible victims of the offender and the offence', as Jimmy Boyle describes them. Though these people can scarcely be called parishioners of the prison chaplain, they deserve to be considered in this chapter, for frequently he has contact with them and sometimes knows them better than their own parochial clergy do.

In the case of an unmarried prisoner especially, parents are caused most distress, not only by separation from their son or daughter but by fears and anxieties about the future: is this to be the beginning of a life of crime? will he or she leave prison less able to cope with life than before? It can be a harrowing experience to have to deal with anguished parents who have done all that could be expected of them to set a good example to their children and to bring them up well, only to find that one of them has now landed up 'inside'.

Occasionally, parental concern can be strangely selective. One woman, whose three older sons had all done time, was, it seemed, inordinately distressed by the fact that the fourth had now followed his elder brothers' example. But the crucial difference was that while the other boys had committed 'respectable crimes' (like 'nicking' and grievous bodily harm), the youngest lad had been sentenced for a sexual offence. As she explained, in words that would have done credit to Mrs Malaprop: 'I can understand John and Jimmy and Joe, but Tommy's different; I'd never have believed that all those years we were nurturing in our family a sexual privet!'

Sometimes the son or daughter will try and ease the parents' concern by concealing from them anything that might cause them anxiety. Jason had made an escape bid and now, like other 'E-men', he had to wear garish yellow patches on the pocket of his jacket and down the sides of his trousers. When his next visit came round, mother wanted to know what he was doing dressed up like that. 'It's nothin', Ma', he assured her, 'stop worryin'.' But her worrying continued; several times during the visit she asked for an explanation of the yellow stripes. Finally, with an air of triumph, Jason pointed to the offending patches and said: 'Look, Ma, I told ya not to worry; if ya really want to know why I'm wearin' this uniform, it's because they've enrolled me in the prison band'. Only Jason could have thought up an excuse like that, and perhaps no one apart from Jason's 'Ma' would have believed it. But she at least went home a happy woman.

However, most prisoners are married and it is their immediate family that are most deeply affected. A home is left without a breadwinner, children without a father, a wife without a husband. All too often, a prisoner's family are regarded by society at large as 'guilty by association': they are looked down upon, treated as though they deserve the hard times they have to face, and, worse still, the extent of their difficulties is simply ignored. Besides the loneliness and emotional frustration, wives feel the strain of making ends meet, of having to seek Social Security ('the most degrading thing that ever happened to me' as one of them put it), of having to be responsible for matters that used to be taken care of by the husband, of having to be both father and mother to their children.

Eighteen years ago a report was published on the social consequences to wives and families of men in prison,[11] and nothing has occurred in the intervening years to invalidate its main conclusions. It draws attention to patterns of behaviour which frequently occur among prisoners' children and which the wives now have to cope with, such as truanting from school, fretting, bed-wetting. Most of the children miss their father and want to have him back or even join him in prison. One little eight-year-old, caught tampering with the doors of a car, explained to the policeman that he was hoping to get arrested so that he could be with his dad. Often enough mothers try to conceal from their children the fact that father is in prison by telling them that he has gone abroad, or is at sea or is 'at school, learning to be clever'. Sometimes they make the extremely painful decision not to allow the children to accompany them on their visits to prison, so that the youngsters may be spared the ordeal of seeing their father in such unhappy surroundings.

What was said in the last chapter about the constraints that attend prison visits applies to wives and families just as much as to the prisoners themselves: the excitement when the visit is in prospect, the depression when it is over; the risk of misunderstandings; the inability to communicate with each other in the way they long to. Moreover, the material circumstances of the visit are often woefully inadequate. Visitors may have to wait outside, whatever the weather, until it is almost time for the visit to begin; but even when they are allowed to enter the prison complex, they may find that conditions there leave much to be desired. This is how Her Majesty's Inspector of Prisons assessed the situation in his report for 1984: 'With some notable exceptions waiting rooms were commonly drab, cheerless and in need of decoration. Facilities for mothers with young children were generally inadequate or non-existent. Visiting rooms were often shabby and poorly ventilated. Refreshments were frequently not available'.[12]

Finally, prisoners' wives are often haunted by uncertainties as to how things will work out when their husbands rejoin them: they have managed so long on their own, will they find it hard to readjust to each other's company? One wife rang up the chaplain a month or so after her husband's release, and, while obviously relieved that they were now reunited, made the telling comment: 'Mind you, it's been a strange experience, almost like getting married again; somehow he seems different and I've got to get to know him afresh. It seems odd having a man about the house when you've been alone so long'.

The better one appreciates the plight of the 'invisible', and innocent, victims, the more one can understand why Pope John Paul II urges us all: 'Do not forget all those with special needs, particularly those who are in prison *and their families*' (italics added).

Parishioners in uniform

Though prisoners are a chaplain's first concern, he has traditionally been regarded – and regards himself – as chaplain to the whole prison community. Prisons are labour-intensive, and the bulk of the labour force is made up of prison officers, over 18,000 of them all told. They are our parishioners, too.

In the previous chapter we considered the effects of prison on the captives, but what about its effects on the captors? After all, the officers spend even longer behind bars than do most of the prisoners; theirs is a life – or, at any rate, a working-life – sentence. If conditions in which inmates live are sometimes appalling, they are the same conditions in which the officers have to work. And their task is made the more difficult not only because of the unpredictability of the difficult men in their care, but also because of the excessively long hours of overtime they work: on average more than sixteen hours each per week.[13]

Inevitably, therefore, they too run the risk of becoming institutionalised. Some appear cynical and obstructive; many are torn by the conflicting demands of discipline and treatment; others are rigid in their attitudes, security-conscious to an extreme degree, suspicious of inmates and administrators and 'do-gooders' such as chaplains; and there are those who look down on prisoners as though they were a lesser breed. An Anglican colleague of mine left at a Wing office the list of men he wanted for a chaplain's discussion group, the name of each man being preceded by 'Mr'. When he picked up the list later, he found that each 'Mr' had been crossed out and at the bottom of the page was scribbled: 'There are no Misters on this Wing, Chaplain'. My friend was strongly tempted to enquire if that included the officer who had penned the message!

In the Peter Sellers film *Two-Way Stretch*, a prison officer is seen roaring at an unfortunate inmate: 'SILENCE when you're talking to me!' I suspect that that portrayal, allowing for its obvious exaggeration, would be in accord with the average outsider's view of prison officers. He sees them as rough, brutal, unreasonable and uncaring. That may be true of some of them: it would be nothing short of miraculous if there were no bad apples in the basket, if, among such a large body of men, there were not some who ought never to have donned an officer's uniform. But, after twenty years of contact with prison officers, I cannot but admire the dedication and professionalism of so many of them, especially when I recall how difficult, and sometimes dangerous, their responsibilities can be.

Two experiments in recent years have shown, alarmingly, how ordinary decent people can easily be persuaded to obey authority figures even when it involves the infliction of considerable pain on others, or to become authoritarian and aggressive when invited to role-play prison guards. In the latter case the experiment had to be brought to a premature end because of the damaging effects it was having on some of the 'prisoners'.[14] Both experiments were performed in laboratory conditions, a far cry from those of the penal system. Nonetheless, they show the dangers inherent in a situation where one group of human beings has another at its mercy, and hint at the psychological pressures which prison officers may experience in daily life. Against that background, the patience and integrity they regularly display are greatly to their credit.

All this, however, is only part of the picture. As has often been said, the officer is the real expert in dealing with prisoners: he is the one who spends more time with them, and at closer quarters, than any other member of staff; he sees them in all their varying moods, has to judge when he can afford to turn a blind eye to their infractions of the rules and when he must be firm and take appropriate action. It is not without justification that the basic relationship between officer and inmate has been described as the key function in a prison, the factor which more than any other determines and establishes the mood of the whole establishment.

Jimmy Boyle could by no means be regarded as well-disposed to the 'screws', and yet he has admitted that it was the small kindness of an officer that marked a turning point in his own prison career. 'One night', he writes, 'as I lay in the far corner of the cell with my eyes shut, thinking, the door opened quickly and a small paper bag was thrown towards me, then the door shut immediately. I was startled and opened the bag to find two small chocolate biscuits. This almost broke my heart. It seems that two of the screws had left to go and do something and the third when seeing this had opened the door and thrown in the biscuits, even though the strict ruling is that no less than three screws must be present when the door is opened. Although it was obviously the human in him why did he do this? It confused the picture, as it brought something human back into me and I would have preferred to think of us all as animals in the one jungle. This guy had no idea what he had done, he would never imagine how this small action caused me so much inner conflict. I didn't ever say anything to him nor him to me, but he had got to me.'[15]

Jimmy Boyle is not the first or the last prisoner to acknowledge that he has had genuine help at the hands of an officer. It is encouraging to note that the staff of Her Majesty's Inspectorate of Prisons, never slow to criticise when necessary, report that at the end of another year (1984) of visiting prisons throughout the country: 'We (the inspectors) were once again impressed with the positive and caring attitude of many of the staff'.[16]

A way of the cross

'I must tell you how much I have benefited from my time with the Prison Service' wrote a part-time chaplain just before his retirement. 'The work is enormously important, something I did not appreciate prior to seeing things from the inside.' I have heard a number of comments like that over the years from people who had got close to prisoners.

It was another clergyman, not a chaplain this time but a priest who took part in a Holy Week Mission in a huge remand prison, who wrote a most moving commentary on his experience.

'I was privileged to be able to keep Holy Week this year with the men in prison. The lives of the men provided the most eloquent backcloth to the Lord's passion that I have ever experienced. Often I was welcomed into a cell. In spite of the overcrowding a space was found for me to sit down. The men were always gentle and courteous. Gladly they would share with me what little they had to offer. A cup of plastic tea, a hoarded biscuit or a thinly rolled cigarette. After such a feast what could I tell them about the upper room?

'Some were deeply hurt because they had been betrayed by someone whom they had trusted. What could I tell these men about the garden?

'Some of the men were very confused. They had been arrested for the first time. On my wing 360 men shared four single toilets. Imagine their feelings as they queue in the morning after spending thirteen hours locked in their cells. These men know how Jesus would have felt in the Praetorium.

'Often they feel useless and helpless. Often they have to depend on total strangers. Someone cooks their meals for them. Someone is preparing their case for them. Everything is done for them by a stranger. As the prison is overcrowded the men sleep three to a cell. Their whole life has to be shared with someone they don't know, someone they did not choose for themselves. It's hard to receive help from total strangers so what could I tell these men about Simon of Cyrene?

'Some men felt deeply ashamed of the trouble they had brought on their families. Often a wife, burdened with the responsibility of looking after the family alone, would travel long distances to visit whenever she could. Visits are one of the few things the men can long for. How can you say all your heart feels in so short a time? Perhaps the wife leaves in tears. The prisoner returns to his cell nursing an even more acute sense of absence and emptiness. There is nothing these men don't know about Mary at the foot of the cross.

'Being in prison is like living under a magnifying glass. There is so much time, but no space, no freedom. Problems are mulled over time and time again but they can never be thought through. One can grow accustomed to physical discomfort, but mental anguish won't go away. What could I tell these men about Calvary?

'Faced with men who knew Christ's suffering so intimately already, what could I do? I just walked about the prison and listened to those who had so much to say. Everyone was so gentle. No-one was ever rude to me. No matter how bitter and resentful a man was, he seemed glad to be able to talk to someone who cared. No matter how degraded or ashamed a man felt, he seemed to be uplifted by a caring ear. No matter how hurt he felt inside himself, my just being there seemed to be the first step on his road to healing.

'Sometimes I went home in the evening feeling totally drained. I don't know why; I had done nothing. It was as if I were carrying out of the gates of the prison some of the hurt felt by the men inside. Looked at in one sense the week was a waste of time. As far as I know no-one was converted. In fact, I spent very little time talking explicitly about God. As I have said, there is nothing I could have told them about the Lord's passion. Perhaps my being there, perhaps my wasting this time with them, perhaps my absorbing some of their hurt, was all I needed to tell them about the Lord's resurrection.'[17]

Even I, who might be regarded as hardened because of the many years I have ministered in prison, find that that meditation touches me very deeply. It reminds me again that in prison we are not just givers but receivers also. And as I think about my prison parishioners, I am ready to make my own these words of Jean Vanier, a deeply spiritual man renowned for his work among the handicapped and a regular visitor to the imprisoned:

> Peace to you, my brothers and sisters.
> Give me some of your strength, your patience, your courage,
> hidden as you are behind the walls
> that I may continue to live for the Kingdom
> and that my hopes never tire.
> Keep me in your heart.[18]

6

PRISON PASTOR

Lord, whatever would become of the prisoner, if Christian society, that is the Church, were to reject him as civil society rejects him? ... There could not be a greater despair than that for the prisoner.

(The Brothers Karamazov)

The Prison Chaplain is the focal point of the Church's ministry to prisoners, and the importance of his work deserves recognition.

(Prisons and Prisoners in England Today: §120)

I slipped back the cover of the judas-hole and glanced into the cell, as I always did before entering. A young man was sitting on the bed, his bowed head in his hands. I could see the tears glistening, as they seeped through his fingers and dripped down upon his overalls, marking the material with tiny dark patches where they fell.

He had just received a 'dear John', a letter from his wife – or was it from his girlfriend? – to say that she had found someone else; it was all over; he wouldn't be seeing her again. It was a scene that seemed to portray the most tragic thing that can happen to a human being: the break-up of a relationship, with the trail of heartache and loneliness and emptiness and frustration that follows in its wake. But, happily, there is a companion scene: the joy and peace, the relief and gladness that fill a man's heart when friendship is restored.

The whole of the Bible might be described in terms of these two scenes, or more precisely of the transformation of the one, alienation, into the other, reconciliation, a process which reaches its climax in the life, death and resurrection of Jesus Christ.

Ambassadors of reconciliation

Jesus came 'to gather together in unity the scattered children of God' (Jn 11:52), to break down the walls of division, so that those 'who once were far off have been brought near through the blood of Christ' (Eph 2:13). His reconciling work is vividly represented by the stark cross silhouetted against the sky above Calvary, its upright reaching towards the heavens, and its cross-beam stretching out like two arms to draw all mankind into its embrace. ' ... in Christ', proclaims St Paul, 'God was reconciling the world to himself.' But that is not all, for Paul continues: '(God was) entrusting to *us* the message of reconciliation. So *we* are ambassadors for Christ, God making his appeal through *us* ... be reconciled to God' (2 Cor 5:18–20: emphasis added).

Those words re-echo in the heart of the prison chaplain. They re-echo also in the hearts of all those – lay and clerical, male and female – who are involved in pastoral work in prison; indeed, much of what is written in this chapter applies to them as much as it does to the official chaplains. When in 1983 an International Commission of Principal Prison Chaplains meeting in Strasbourg drew up a 'Charter for Prison Chaplains', they summed up the prison ministry in terms of reconciliation: 'The prison chaplaincy tries to offer help and support to prisoners by assisting their human and spiritual development and to accompany them on their way towards reconciliation with themselves, with others and with God'.[1]

Reconciliation with oneself: On several occasions already reference has been made to the poor self-image that many prisoners have, a self-image which they feel is confirmed by the deeds that have brought them into prison. In 1985 Prisoners Week took as its theme 'Focus on Forgiveness', calling upon Christians everywhere to respond to our Lord's daunting command to show forgiveness to those who have hurt us and our loved ones. An ex-prisoner, interviewed for the *Sunday* programme on Radio 4, was asked how he thought prisoners would react to that theme. They would be very puzzled, he thought, because 'most of them can't even forgive themselves'.

The chaplain tries to help his people to come to terms with themselves and accept themselves as they really are, so that, on the one hand, they may have courage to recognise their sinfulness, while being confident of the boundless mercy of God towards all who repent; and, on the other, be able to recognise their good qualities and strive to build on them for the future. The chaplain's task is often a difficult one. 'My first Christmas in the prison apostolate' one chaplain wrote, 'has left me with an indelible memory, the memory of a man who could not cope with his personal guilt. He held a responsible position in a well-known school, and had been charged with indecent assault on one of the pupils. He admitted several other crimes of a similar nature and was located in conditions meant to preserve his personal safety. While all grades of staff acted with complete professionalism, the longer he was locked up the more depressed he became. His family disowned him and I spent many hours just talking to him and trying to reassure him that all was not lost. On Christmas Eve I got permission from the Governor to stay on later so that

I could spend more time with him. Before I left we said a prayer which asked for courage and strength for this tortured man, and ended with an act of sorrow. I left him a little prayerbook and wished him God's blessing. I arrived very early on Christmas morning because there was much to prepare, but first, I thought, I must visit my friend. When I opened the door, there he was hanging against the wall by the cell-window, having used his sheet as a noose. He left me a note in the prayerbook, telling me how much he had tried and asking me to pray for his soul and all those he had hurt by his crime.'

That may read like a tale of failure, but the Lord has an uncanny knack of drawing glorious victory out of what seems to be defeat. I cannot but believe that that unhappy man has finally found the reconciliation with himself that he longed for.

Reconciliation with others: Crime, as we have seen, has far-reaching effects: the victim, the criminal, the family and friends of both, are all caught up in the tragedy. The wrong-doer himself is often only too well aware that he has a great deal of 'making up' to do. And for his part, the chaplain aims to promote whatever will help him to rebuild damaged relationships, behave with a greater sense of responsibility towards others and do what he can to make amends to those whom he has hurt.

At times the prisoner needs little encouragement. A youngish man, who had killed both his common-law wife and his daughter in circumstances of such provocation that he was found guilty of manslaughter rather than murder, told me his story without any attempt to minimise his own responsibility, and it was clear that the concern uppermost in his mind was the fate of his loved ones. 'They were – well, you know – not very good women in some ways, but I still love them. And now I've killed them, and they've gone before God without a chance to get ready to meet him. Do you think they'll be in heaven? Will you pray for them?'

I could see the relief in his eyes, as I gently reminded him that God loved Jean and Jennie even more than he did. As for the prayer, we knelt down there and then, and prayed together for forgiveness, for the eternal rest of the two women, and for himself that he would accept the pains of his imprisonment as penance for what he had done. That was not quite the end of the story. In the course of the next few months I discovered that, in addition to morning and night prayers, he would spend a whole hour in prayer each day, and I know that as he went before the Lord the names of Jean and Jennie were often on his lips.

One of the most frightening features of prison life is the amount of healing that needs to be done; there is so much hurt, so much bitterness and hatred about, sometimes directed against people, parents perhaps or school teachers, for ill-treatment meted out long ago; sometimes directed against prison officers or other prisoners or society at large. The chaplain at one of our biggest local prisons has written a report on the remarkable results that were achieved by a three-day Mission, led by a priest who is long experienced in the ministry of healing.

It was not simply that the services were very well attended, but that an almost palpable change took place in the whole atmosphere of the prison. One of the congregation used to return to his cell after every service, and write down with bewildering accuracy almost every word the missioner had spoken, so that he could reflect upon it later and share it with other men who, for one reason or another, had not been present.

Reconciliation with God: In an interview for radio I was once asked what I regarded as the main purpose of the chaplain's work in prison. To my eternal discredit, I went a complete blank and found myself muttering something about the necessity of keeping the Church alive to its responsibilities for the imprisoned. I would not of course wish to deny that that is part of his brief, but I am sure that the main purpose of his ministry is to try to convince prisoners that God loves them. If he can do that, nothing else matters very much, or, rather, if he can do that everything else that matters will follow. It is particularly in the prison world that the powerful gospel message of God's acceptance of us despite our unacceptability has to be proclaimed: in the moment that a man is able to accept that acceptance 'grace conquers sin, and reconciliation bridges the gulf of estrangement'.[2]

A prisoner who spent many years in Dartmoor was befriended by the Methodist chaplain and recovered the Christian faith of his youth. He proved the genuineness of his conversion over a lengthy period and shortly after his release was invited to address the Methodist Penal Affairs Conference. He had had no previous experience of public speaking, but his obvious sincerity earned him the attention and, finally, the applause of his audience. Afterwards at dinner he found himself flanked, as he expressed it, 'by the high and the mighty', on the one side the Deputy Director General of the Prison Service and on the other a senior prison governor. (It was hard to believe that only a few weeks earlier he had been 237190 Bloggs.) Some days later he accompanied the chaplain to an ecumenical service. He listened attentively to a passage from the letter to the Galatians in which Paul describes how in Christ the barriers that divide people have been thrown down, so that there is no longer Jew and Gentile, slave and freeman, male and female; then, turning to the chaplain, he said in an excited stage whisper: 'He's talking about what happened to *me*, isn't he?'

A small yet moving example of the reconciling work of the chaplaincy is to be found in a prayer group which was set up in a 'lifers' wing in 1981, as the result of an ecumenical retreat in which the chaplains of the institution tried to discover, through prayer and discussion, what were God's plans for them. It was launched by two of the chaplaincy, one a Methodist minister, the other a Roman Catholic Sister, and has met weekly ever since, with attendances varying between four and seventeen. This is how one of its present members sees its value: 'It's a kind of anchor for us in the wing. There are all kinds of barriers to be broken down still ... we are becoming less suspicious. Three of us can pray together in a cell only because we trust one another from the group. At first I shuddered when I had to sit with others ... I wanted to close up. Now it doesn't matter ... the atmosphere in the wing is changing'.

Perhaps the ripples of reconciliation extend even further than that prisoner imagined. Though officers do not take part in the meetings, the Sister recalls: 'Singing is very important in our prayer group, and it isn't unusual to hear a prison officer humming our hymns afterwards. On one occasion an officer actually asked that we should sing a hymn of his choice during our meeting'. Reconciliation, as we have seen, has three facets – it affects an individual's attitude to himself, to his neighbour and to God – and it is not surprising that progress in one area is often accompanied by corresponding advances in the other two.

Priests, pastors and prophets

In accomplishing his reconciling work, Jesus has traditionally been viewed as prophet, priest and king. Since the prison chaplain shares in that reconciling work, it may be useful to view him in similar fashion. But of course a king is hardly the kind of person you would expect to meet in a prison, and anyway the word 'king' has a special significance in the Scriptures – even in Old Testament times the king was spoken of as shepherd-king, and in the New Testament *the* King, Jesus himself, is 'the good Shepherd', the pastor ever at the service of his flock, ready to wash their feet and even to lay down his life for them – and so let us say that the chaplain in his reconciling work fills the three-fold role of priest, prophet and pastor.

Priest

One of the finest pieces of advice I ever received came from a wise old parishioner who had heard that I was to become a prison chaplain. She simply said: 'Remember, father, that the most important thing about a *prison* priest is that he is a prison *priest*'. She was right. The prison chaplain may pass most of his working hours in rather strange surroundings and have a pretty unusual bunch of parishioners, but his essential role is the same as that of the parish priest or vicar or minister in the world outside. He will get involved in a great deal of welfare work, he will counsel, he may feel the need to brush up his knowledge of the social sciences, but primarily he is not psychologist or probation officer or social worker or professional counsellor; he is priest. Like the parish clergy, he has been called to preach the good news, to lead his people in worship, to hold up his little community before the Father in prayer, to celebrate the sacraments. The Eucharist is, in the words of Vatican II, the summit to which all the other activities of the week are leading and the source from which they all flow.[3]

The chaplain might be described as a frontiersman: even if he is full-time, he does not really 'belong' to the establishment; he comes from outside, his roots – and they are deep and sturdy – lie in the Church. He has a part to play, therefore, in opening up the establishment to the community, linking the 'little islands' to the 'mainland'; and, perhaps even more importantly, in bringing something of the outside world into prison, introducing a measure of normality into the artificial world 'inside'. There are some prisoners who claim that the chapel is the one place in prison where they feel that they are something more than simply prisoners. 'I stand here in chapel', said one man at the beginning of a six-year sentence, 'I am not really a religious fellow, but I know when I am in here that I matter.' Another expressed it by a simple but picturesque analogy when he wrote: 'Coming to chapel? It is like having a headache all week, and then you take an aspirin, and it all goes away for a while'.

The expression of such sentiments indicates that prison chapels have a special symbolic value of their own. Most of them are worthy buildings, some quite beautiful, but all of them are meant to speak of hope, of human dignity and the essential equality of all human beings, of resurrection, and of love. When a new chapel was opened at Warren Hill in Suffolk in 1982 the then Minister of the Prison Department sent this message to the chaplaincy: 'God is love ... Love cannot be contained ... Love is the freedom of prisoners. It is the gift due *to* all men *from* all men. Some of us are specially called to impart that gift. This chapel, therefore, is in truth at the heart of this institution. Without it the order we pursue is barren. With it, it is endowed with a constructive and holy purpose. Our prayers must be that those who come here may go forth strengthened and made more complete'.

Services in prison chapels have a special place in my memory. Some of them, like the beautiful celebrations we had at Easter and Christmas – when the chapel would be wonderfully decorated and a group of outsiders (my own mother among them, on several occasions) would be present – stirred me in a way that few church services have ever done. Though prison congregations can be unpredictable in their behaviour, my abiding recollection is of their attentiveness, their at times uncanny stillness. More than once when celebrating Sunday Mass 'outside' I have been mildly shocked by the amount of noise, the number of distractions, the lack of listening, all of which compared so unfavourably with what I had become accustomed to 'inside'. There is, however, one way in which a prison congregation is unique: it is single-sexed, and that is why my Sunday celebrations brought home to me in a way that nothing else did the bizarre nature of a community of captives: in the prison chapel you never (or hardly ever) see a woman, never witness the antics of small children, never hear a baby's cry. This is a phoney world.

A prison chaplain, recognising that his men and women are themselves 'a priestly people' (1 Peter 2:5, 9), is anxious to involve them as much as possible in chapel worship: as readers, as altar servers, as bearers of the offertory gifts. Despite coaching, prison readers can sometimes give an unintended twist of humour to a scriptural passage. So, we heard several times of 'The Letter to the Philippines', and, in Liverpool prison, the venerable gentlemen Eldad and Medad, upon whom the Spirit descended (Nums 11:24–30), became 'Eldad an' me dad'! But one of the lovely things about a prison congregation, unlike the more staid and self-conscious ones outside, is that its members feel free to laugh aloud – even if the laugh is on themselves. I had put into phonetical spelling the word 'licentiousness', which was causing some bother to a reader-to-be. He asked me what the word meant, and, having got his answer, replied slowly – using his phonetic version with great care – 'LIE-SENT-CHUS-NESS? I may not be able to say it well, but I bet I know more about it than you do!'

It is in worship, in word and sacrament, that reconciliation is sometimes achieved in surprising ways. Albert was one of the toughest lads I ever met: he had been soldiering for many years in every quarter of the globe and was still ready to offer his services as a mercenary to anyone who would pay him the right price. He had not practised his religion since leaving school, but was eventually appointed as my 'red-band' sacristan. We got to know each other well; we talked for hours and he began to say his prayers but maintained that he could never return to the sacraments. At first, though he prepared the altar to perfection, he would hide in the vestry during the worship itself. After a while, he found courage to take part in services, but he still insisted that he was far too bad to be ever again a real practising Christian.

Good Friday came round and I led the men in the liturgy of the Passion, which in the Roman rite includes the veneration of the cross. In this ceremony the congregation is invited to approach the large crucifix, which has been solemnly unveiled, and venerate this symbol of the Master's suffering by kissing the feet transpierced by a nail. Albert was there, but, as I had anticipated, did not take part in the act of veneration. When the service was over, I quizzed him gently: 'Great to see you here, today, Bert. I notice you didn't go up to kiss the crucifix with the other lads. Can you remember what you were doing then?' 'Oh yes', came the unexpected reply, 'I know exactly what I was doing. I was just looking at Jesus in all his sufferings, and I was saying to him as hard as I could: "Jesus, forgive me; forgive me for all the rotten lousy things I've done to you".' I said nothing; I could only recall that our Lord had spoken of joy in heaven over even one sinner that repents.

It is especially that kind of event which reminds the prison chaplain that like the high priest of former times 'he himself is beset by weakness and so must make offerings for himself as well as for the people' (Heb 5:2–3). If the first part of Karl Rahner's address to prison chaplains (see pages 9–10) was concerned with finding Christ in prisoners, the second was concerned with finding ourselves in them. 'We find ourselves in the prisoners when we see in them the hidden truth of our own situation. The truth that we are sinners; the truth that we are self-seekers; the truth that in a thousand different ways, crude or subtle, we are always trying to serve God *and* ourselves; ... We may be free in a bourgeois, legal sense: we may be responsible for our actions, not only in the sight of men but also in the sight of God ... But if we have not been set free by the Spirit of God ... we are nevertheless helpless and hopeless prisoners in the prison of our guilt, our unsaved condition, our inability to perform any saving act.' And he adds the pointed reflection: 'When you go from your own surroundings into a prison, you do not go out of a world of harmony, light and order into a world of guilt and unfreedom: you stay where you have been all the time. It is merely made clearer to your bodily senses what has been surrounding you all the time'.[4]

Pastor

Though the prison chapel is the chaplain's special 'scene', his area of responsibility extends far beyond the chapel door: in fact to every corner of the prison. Like any other priest, he is by definition *pastor*, shepherd of the flock entrusted to him. And so, just as the clergyman in a parish goes to welcome new arrivals, the prison chaplain normally begins his day 'inside' by going – well, not to welcome exactly, but – to receive with friendship his new parishioners and offer them whatever help he can. It would be hard to overestimate the significance of this meeting with 'receptions', the first time he is able to meet the newcomers, but, even more importantly, the first time that they have the opportunity of meeting him. First impressions may be lasting ones; often there is a good deal of hurt about – fresh, raw hurt – which must be handled with tact and care; this man may be longing for someone in whom he can confide, someone who can help him to handle his guilt or to re-establish links with his family; he should be able to find in this chaplain the reassuring sign that whatever he may have done, however he may have been rejected by others, he is no outcast so far as the Church and still more so far as Christ himself is concerned. An example of how beautifully this can happen is borne out by a former prisoner who wrote to his chaplain, perhaps with pardonable exaggeration: 'One lepper (*sic*) returns to say thanks. Thank you for what you did and for your kindness in a sea of inhumanity'.

The clergyman in a parish visits his people in their homes, and so too the prison chaplain tries to visit his people systematically in *their* homes, which for the time being happen to be drab, dismal prison cells. It is impressive to read Ezechiel's account of his pastoral ministry to the prisoners in Babylon: ... I came to them of the captivity ... and I sat where they sat' (3:14–15). The prison chaplain, like a true pastor, tries to reach out to his people wherever they may be, and to sit where they sit both physically and psychologically: to take them where they are, to try and see things through their eyes, to listen to them to share their interests, to respect them, to offer them the hand of friendship. '(The offer of friendship), theologically speaking, is redemptive', writes Gregory Baum, 'For the agape-love which a Christian extends to a troubled person touches him with a gesture of Christ himself (even if his name should remain unmentioned) rendering possible the remaking of life.'[5] Even where the friendship knows tragedy, it still may accompany a person to his death. A chaplain recalls a young man, mentally disordered and awaiting a medical report before being tried, who left a suicide note for the priest in which he wrote: 'I never knew why you wanted to be my friend and when you came to visit me in my cell and sat on my bed with me, I really wanted to talk to you, but I couldn't ... I know you'll understand'.

Just as the clergyman outside has a special care for the sick and for those who have met with misfortune, so the prison pastor makes his daily call upon those of his parishioners who are in the prison hospital and those who are in solitary confinement. For them particularly the days can be very long, and niggling anxieties assume gigantic proportions. Almost without exception he is well received, though that does not necessarily mean that those who receive him are gospel-hungry: they may simply want a visitor, or a helper, or someone they can manipulate. Sometimes a prisoner who has just been 'weighed off' (that is, adjudicated upon for an infringement of prison rules) can be in a pretty volatile condition. An Anglican colleague of mine, who called on such a man, received a straight left to the jaw which sent him reeling out of the cell, grey-faced and shaken. How I admired him for the way he returned the same evening to visit the same cell. I was not surprised to learn that there was a genuine apology awaiting him and an explanation that the punch was not meant specifically for him but 'for the first one who came to that ruddy door'. Perhaps part of the reconciling work of the pastor is to be willing to soak up without complaint some of the hostility and anger that hang about a prison like mustard gas.

A ready repartee and a sense of humour need to be used with care but they can prove invaluable allies in the right circumstances. A chaplain, who had had great difficulties with a particularly awkward young man on the punishment block, forgot to pass a word of warning to the clergyman who was acting as his substitute. The latter blithely opened the cell-door with a cheery greeting, only to be met with a snarling: 'I don't have to talk to s..t'. The answer came back like a bullet: 'Lucky you, I *do* have to'. The young man's angry face began to crumble into a smile. Within seconds there was a guffaw of laughter, and before long the barriers between prisoner and chaplain had tumbled down completely.

Like any other clergyman, the prison chaplain has to face the difficult pastoral task of counselling those suffering bereavement or facing other tragedies. But, for him, the task is made so much more onerous by the circumstances in which it has to be carried out. He is usually the one who has to break the sad news in the first place. What do you say to a man who has just heard that his wife has been killed in a road accident, and who will not be allowed home until the day of the funeral, and who has to depend upon others to make all the arrangements? How do you console someone who has been shattered to learn that his child is seriously ill, and who in the loneliness of his cell is tormented by anxiety as to what may happen and frustration at being unable to do anything or even to be with his dear ones in their sufferings? However, a chaplain may discover that in situations like that the real pastor to the hurt individual will not be himself but the prisoner who is sharing the cell. He is the one who will stay awake half the night, talking to his cell-mate, listening to him, and understanding him as perhaps no chaplain ever could.

Indeed, one of the duties of a pastor is to discover and promote the pastoral gifts of others. In a recent article a former chaplain describes how, once he had begun work in prison, 'It soon became apparent, that it was the preached who were doing the preaching, the imprisoned who were doing the liberating. Michael, in his early thirties, wrote to me on the eve of his leaving prison. In the letter he explained how for the past ten years he had been in and out of prisons. He hadn't thought seriously of changing his life style. "Your words" he said "made me stop and think, but I don't imagine they would have made all that much difference if it hadn't been for Paddy". (Paddy was an old alcoholic constantly in prison for shoplifting.) "I was two-ed up with Paddy", Michael went on. "He went to Mass every Sunday, so I started to go. He knelt down every night and said his prayers, so I started to do the same."' He concludes: 'Jimmy and Paddy were not exceptional, I met scores of such men in prison'.[6] Most prison chaplains could say the same.

Finally, just as his confrère in a parish runs meetings and clubs for his people, so the prison chaplain tries to organise various group activities for his people. It may be a discussion group, or a Scripture study course, or a choir practice, or even, as indicated earlier, a braille class. In all this, and indeed in and through all his other pastoral work, the chaplain finds himself caught up in a whirlpool of other tasks, from counselling a couple whose marriage is on the point of disaster to ringing up a neighbour to enquire if a man's budgie is being cared for while he is 'inside'. But for the most part it is that 'active helpfulness', spoken of by Dietrich Bonhoeffer, which consists in a multitude of deeds, tiny and apparently trifling in themselves, yet very much at the heart of Christian service. He must be adept at what has been finely described as 'loitering with intent', simply being there and being available. It is small wonder that a questionnaire distributed among chaplains in these islands and on the continent, revealed that 'the greatest problem in their ministry', so far as part-time chaplains are concerned, is 'lack of time: in comparison with that all other difficulties pale into insignificance'. In a report to their bishops in 1980, the prison chaplains of Ireland, North and South, underline 'the inability of part-time chaplains to spend much time with prisoners' and commented that experience had shown that attendance at services and reception of sacraments 'is directly related to the quality of the relationship between the chaplain and the prisoner. This can only be achieved through time spent with individual prisoners'.[7]

Of course, there are some respects in which the pastor in prison differs markedly from his opposite number in a parish outside. Surely he is the only one who would like to be out of a job, who rejoices to see his parishioners leaving him; even hopes and prays that they will never grace his chapel again, though he realises that even that modest ambition will not be realised in many cases. Another unique aspect of the chaplain's work – as mentioned already in regard to his priestly ministry – is that he is a frontiersman: within the institution, but not altogether of it, part of the system but apart from it, chaplain and pastor to the inmates but also to the staff. It is a delicate path to tread; his first concern is for prisoners and yet if he becomes exclusively a 'cons' man', not only is he cutting off the staff and their families from his pastoral activity, he is also alienating the very ones who can do so much to help him in his work. And of course if he is seen simply as 'the screws' man', then he might as well stay outside the prison altogether. As best he may, he must aim to become 'all things to all men', and it is very refreshing to meet a man who has achieved that, who has proved himself a first-rate prisoners' pastor, but who tells you with conviction: 'If a month goes by without a member of staff weeping on my shoulder, I know it's time to examine my conscience'.

There is so much more to say about the pastoral ministry of the chaplain, but it would be hard to find a neater summary of his shepherding role than in these lines, written by an American bishop for the clergy of his diocese: 'People are not looking for religious leaders who can solve all their problems or answer all their questions. More than anything else, people look to us who minister to them for our presence as loving, caring, and forgiving people. They want our help in their efforts to handle pain and frustration. They look to us for understanding; they seek a sensitive and consoling response to their hurt feelings; they need the spiritual comfort we can bring through our ministry of word and sacrament. They want someone who will pray with them, whose presence will remind them that, no matter what their difficulties might be, God really loves them and cares for them.'[8]

Prophet

If the chaplain is a frontiersman between the prison world and the 'outside' world, and between prisoners and staff, he is also, in a sense, a frontiersman between earth and heaven. He is a prophet, one called to speak the word of God to the prison situation. His very presence should help to keep alive what Peter Berger has called 'the rumour of angels', even within the dark and complex world of a penal institution his activities are 'signs of transcendence'[9] he is a living reminder that there is a spiritual dimension in human beings that it is dangerous to ignore, that institutions like individuals must be guided by moral considerations, that the facile distinctions made between prisoners and staff receive no recognition from the Father of all mankind. Perhaps it was an appreciation of the prophetic role of the chaplain that led a prisoner to say: 'If there should come a time when a chaplain no longer enters the prisons, it'll be time for the gas chambers to be built'. And if a prisoner's view should be regarded as jaundiced, then what is to be made of a prison governor who has said on more than one occasion: 'As I pass through my institution day after day I have constantly to remind myself that there is only one step between a prison and a concentration camp'? In less emotive language, another governor said that he saw the chaplain as 'the conscience of the institution', the one who draws us all back to basic moral issues, who, along with other specialists such as doctors and teachers and probation officers, has his own particular insights and understandings to contribute towards the well-being of the whole prison community.

Of course, like any other 'conscience', the chaplain may have to be very inconvenient at times: it is instructive to notice how governors sometimes say of a chaplain – often with a disarming smile: 'Who will rid me of this turbulent priest?' I wish to suggest that our institutions might be that much worse if there were not such turbulent clerics, such awkward prophets, about – and perhaps a good deal better if there were even more of them who were even more turbulent.

Like the prophets, those 'stirrers of conscience' in ancient Israel – and 'stirrer of conscience' is a rather more accurate description of what the chaplain is called to be – prison clergy are often misunderstood: staff may dismiss them as well-meaning but irrelevant and ineffective; inmates may regard them as being in the pocket of the governor and not to be trusted. Such misunderstandings within the prison community are understandable enough – on some occasions at least they are richly deserved – but with the passage of time they can also be modified as staff and inmates come to know their chaplain better. What are much more painful are the misunderstandings which sometimes exist within the Christian community outside. It is hard to hear a Christian, especially if he or she has no first-hand experience of prison, criticising prison chaplains because, for example, they sit on boards, or carry keys, or make reports, or take the Official Secrets Act, and, in a rather superior way, accusing them of betraying their position.

Such critics seem to suffer from the Pontius Pilate syndrome: at all costs they must keep their hands clean, and would like everybody else to do the same, despite the fact that prisons are a communal responsibility, a responsibility that cannot be shuffled off simply by avoiding all close contact with the penal system. In this context I like to think of our Lord choosing to lay his hands upon the 'defiling' skin of the leper, though he might just as easily have cured him at a distance. The Incarnation is all about not keeping hands clean; it is about getting mixed up in the mess and dirt and greyness of human existence, about trying to be a voice for the voiceless ones even though your motives may be misunderstood and your integrity called into question.

A chaplain takes the Official Secrets Act because that is a condition of his working in a prison. He may wish that it were otherwise, he may realise that it will be misunderstood by some; but he also knows that it is in some ways a protection for prisoners, a safeguard of their privacy, and, more importantly, he knows that in no real sense of the word can it be described as a gagging of himself. It does not threaten his prophetic role, for it leaves him free to pursue issues through internal Prison Department channels: far from being silenced, he is in fact given access to complaint procedures that would otherwise be beyond his reach. Moreover, it is not a question of his being prevented from revealing dire secrets unknown to the world at large. Apart from the confidential knowledge he has about individual prisoners, there is very little he knows that cannot be read by anyone in their daily newspapers.

If he does not find insuperable difficulties in taking the Official Secrets Act, still less does he find them in the carrying of keys. Naturally, he finds it distasteful to be bearing on his person the symbols of captivity – that is why he tries to carry them discreetly, without any ostentatious length of chain dangling down his leg – and he realises that some people will regard him as a 'screw in a Roman collar'. But he knows better: he knows that keys open doors, as well as close them; he knows that those keys, jangling at his side, are like a passport, giving him access to his parishioners wherever they may be throughout the length and breadth of the prison. He knows that without them his pastoral and prophetic work would be severely handicapped.

Finally, there are the writing of reports and the membership of boards. These are perhaps more contentious issues. I know excellent chaplains who refuse to do either because they feel that it compromises their 'neutrality', puts them on the side of the institution, gives them too much power. On the other hand I also know fine chaplains who take a different point of view. One of them sums up his position pithily by saying, 'Look, I'd be prepared to play poker with Satan, so long as I know I could win the last trick'. In more expansive mood, he will explain that attending a Heads of Department meeting or a Regime Board meeting gives him the ideal opportunity of being prophetic, of feeding into the discussions his own theological insights. And as for parole reports, he points out that many prisoners actually ask their chaplains to speak up for them in this way; when faced with the possibility, he says, of being able to help a chap to get back to his wife and kids a little sooner by means of parole, do you think I ought to hold back because of scruples about being contaminated by the system? I do not attempt to answer him, partly because I know that he, like the chaplain who takes a different line, deserves respect, and partly because I find myself drawn to his line of reasoning.

In 1978 when the modern Prison Service was celebrating its hundredth birthday, the Director General attended the annual chaplains' conference and delivered an address in which he declared: 'No organisation created by man to deal with men can be anything but imperfect. We try to improve … as best we can but we know we are going to be found wanting and this is where the chaplains make their distinctive contribution – we need them to point out to us where we are deficient in humanity. We need chaplains in our prisons to help us put a human face on what we are trying to do … '. I hope that he was not merely suggesting that chaplains give a kind of respectability to the prison system, but rather indicating the moral influence they bring to bear, in the sense that a moral philosopher could speak of morality as making and keeping human life really human.[10] And so, allowing for centenary euphoria, I believe that the Director General was paying genuine tribute to the priestly, pastoral and prophetic role of chaplains as they strive to continue the reconciling work of their Master in prison.

Back to basics

In an interview on the radio, a prisoner who had rediscovered the importance of prayer in his life explained that prison gives you plenty of time to get back to basics. That is true not only for prisoners but for their chaplains, also. Whenever I have had the privilege of speaking at the induction course for new chaplains, I have pointed out that clergy are not immune to the institutionalising effects of prison, and yet nothing could be worse than a chaplain who has succumbed to the system, who has become uninterested and heartless, an establishment man. However, I have suggested, if we are to avoid this happening in the pressurised atmosphere in which we pass so many hours of our lives, we must be prepared to return to basics: not so much to our three Rs as our four Ss.

First of all the chaplain must have *sincerity*. He has to earn his place in the prison world: he cannot take it for granted. Prisoners tend to be suspicious of people they do not know; and, to make matters worse, many of them have had unhappy experiences with authority figures. They hate hypocrisy and quickly sniff it out. They want to know what the chaplain is in the job for: because his bishop did not give him the option? because he is after the money? because he thinks it will be easier to get a congregation 'inside'? or because he really cares for them? And if the latter, how does he show it? Though he may not realise it, he is 'on trial': he is going to have to prove himself.

When I had been in the Prison Service only a matter of weeks, I unlocked a cell door and, even before it was pushed open, was surprised to hear the inmate greeting me: 'Hello, father!' and then, as I came into view: 'Yes, I knew it was you'. 'You knew it was me? How did you know it was me?' I asked. 'It was the way you opened the door. Ya know, the screws make an almighty row as though they was tryin' to go straight through the bleedin' thing; but you did it all gentle like'. Little did he realise that the gentleness was motivated more by fear than by consideration! But it taught me from the start the valuable lesson that small things would mean a great deal in trying to build up relationships in prison.

Secondly, and this follows from what has just been explained, the chaplain must be *steadfast*; must be reliable, dependable, for only then can prisoners really trust him and be sure that he is on their side. If he says he will do something, then he must do it. It is an ex-prisoner who makes the point: 'Out there one has freedom of movement and expression. In here we are so helpless that it's doubly important that the few promises ever made to us should be honoured'.[11]

A chaplain must be steadfast, too, in sticking to his task, despite the heavy demands it makes on him, and despite his apparent lack of success. It was a wise Chaplain General who used often to remind us that 'success' is a word unknown in the vocabulary of the New Testament. And yet, as Bishop Taylor insists, there is a great danger that for modern Christians, ' ... in a madly competitive world ... incompetence causes us more shame than sin. Success is the only credential we know ... This makes us ... nervously anxious about the effectiveness of our proclamation of the gospel. The prophets and the apostles were obsessed by divine revelation or the lack of it; we are obsessed by human response or the lack of it'.[12]

It would be idle to suggest that the chaplain is not a prey to such an un-Christian way of thinking, and yet there is a sense in which, more than anyone else in the Prison Service, he should be able to stick to his job in a spirit of optimism. He realises that what he is ultimately trying to do – not to reduce recidivism but help his prison flock to draw closer to our Lord – and the extent to which that is achieved, may well coincide to a far greater degree than the visible evidence would seem to suggest. For 'grace builds on nature', the theologians assure us, and given the backgrounds and temperaments and experiences of so many of our parishioners grace often gets off to a pretty poor start. We can safely leave the Lord to take all that into account.

Thirdly, the chaplain must have *sensitivity*. Sensitivity to the pressures and influences at work in the prison, sensitivity to the demands of security, to the problems of staff (remembering that they are real people who may have problems and difficulties of their own), sensitivity to the frustrations and anxieties of prisoners, sensitivity to the grim home-life that lies behind so many of them, sensitivity to what prison may be doing to himself: he, too, can become callous and cynical and uncaring;

sensitivity to what others may think of his work: it was certainly pretty disconcerting to be told by a well-meaning officer: 'Father, you're wasting your time. I thought there was supposed to be a shortage of priests. You'd be far better off somewhere else'.

High-ranking clerics are not always the most sensitive of people in prison. One of them arrived in a cell doorway and proclaimed: 'What a lovely view you have from here, young man'. 'Mate, you may see the view', replied the prisoner, 'I can only see the bars.' To see a view and not the bars in a prisoner's cell is the height of insensitivity, though to see them both and sensitively share the total vision can be a great blessing.

A much more encouraging episode occurred when a bishop, renowned for his heart of gold and short-fuse temper, was being taken round by a prison chaplain and was invited to have a chat with a lad on the punishment block. As the door was opened, they met a torrent of abuse, the gist of it being that he was on punishment for fighting over a Bible and didn't want 'no more Bible-preachers coming to see me'. The chaplain was horrified; the bishop took it all in his stride. He grasped the lad's hand and told the chaplain to leave them on their own for a while. When he returned, he found bishop and borstal boy sitting on the bed, smoking, with more than the suspicion of a tear in the young lad's eyes. The bishop grinned, as he said by way of explanation: 'We found we both have difficulty in keeping our tempers. So, you see, we understand one another'.

Finally, and most obvious of all, the chaplain must have *spirituality*. It is simply pointless a clergyman going into prison unless he is to be recognisable as God's man – not by any holier-than-thou, pietistic mannerisms, but by the quiet, unpretentious impression he leaves behind him that his way of acting, of living, of talking, of treating others simply would not make sense without a profound commitment to the Lord. It was G. K. Chesterton who once wrote: 'Loving means to love that which is unlovable, or it is no virtue at all; forgiving means to pardon the unpardonable, or it is no virtue at all; faith means believing the unbelievable, or it is no virtue at all; and hope means hoping when things are hopeless, or it is no virtue at all'. In prison life there can be a fair amount of loving the unlovable, pardoning the unpardonable, believing the unbelievable, hoping in the hopeless. I am not unduly naive, but I simply do not believe that we can have the power to do these 'impossible' things unless we strive to live close to the Lord of the Impossible, 'by loving the Lord, ... by heeding his voice, and by holding fast to him' (Deut 30:20) as we continue our reconciling work.

Since the majority of those touched by the work of reconciliation are men and women who have been found guilty of crime, a chaplain who takes his calling seriously feels the need to learn what he can from the criminologists, the experts in the scientific study of crime, and then to reflect upon that in the light of Christian principles. The material of the next chapter is the result of just such a process of learning and reflecting.

7

FOCUSING ON CRIME

In pastoral care, appropriate use must be made not only of theological principles, but also of the findings of psychology and sociology.

(Vatican II)[1]

The heart of man is more devious than any other thing ...
who can pierce its secrets?

(Jeremiah 17:19)

It is tempting to suggest that the first criminological question ever asked was that which was put by the Lord God to Eve, as he walked in the garden in the cool of the evening: '(Eve), what is this you have done?' (Gen 3:13). Despite its form, it was not simply a request for information, but a demand for explanation; it was not just a what-question, it was also a why-question. And ever since that day, one might say, criminology has never looked back.

Over twenty years ago Professor Terence Morris was writing 'that of all the specialised branches of inquiry into social behaviour, criminology has grown at a prodigious rate over the last decade'.[2] That growth has not abated since. And the work of the specialists has been accompanied by the ever-increasing anxiety of the general public. According to recent opinion polls, 'law and order' ranks with unemployment as a major cause for general concern. The person-in-the street wants to know why the crime rate has risen relentlessly since the mid-fifties, and, at least in more thoughtful moments, why it is that some people turn to crime and others do not. The chaplain 'inside' shares these anxieties, but in an even more insistent way he wants to try and understand criminals, because they are his parishioners and he cares for them. He feels he owes it to them to enquire whether the professional criminologists and theologians can throw any light on criminal behaviour. The answers are both intriguing and disappointing, as will be seen in this chapter, which summarises theories advanced by the experts and offers some reflections from a Christian point of view.

Theories of crime

Some years ago, while preparing a brief paper on 'Criminology since World War II', I happened to overhear an argument between a couple of Liverpool prisoners, which ended with the unanswerable riposte: 'Mate, if brains was made of rubber, you wouldn't 'ave enuff rubber to make a pair of flip-flops for a budgie!' Even as I rocked with laughter, I found myself thinking: 'Well, brains apart, my problem is rather different from yours, mate: not a shortage of material but a superabundance of it'.

It is obviously impossible in a few pages to do justice to the many theories of crime that have been propounded over the past two centuries. Inevitably, therefore, I shall have to be selective, and to simplify.

The 'classical' theory of crime

We can take up the story in the second half of the eighteenth century with what came to be known as the Classical (or liberal) school. It arose from the philosophy of the Enlightenment which swept across Europe at that time; it bitterly opposed prevailing legal systems which were hopelessly inadequate, and punishments which were arbitrary and often barbarous. Its main tenets were summed up in the work of a young Italian nobleman philosopher, the Marquis Cesare Beccaria, in his famous *Essay on Crimes and Punishment* which was published in 1764 and had an enormous influence upon penal reformers, including Jeremy Bentham and John Howard.[3] The classical school argued that the law should restrict the 'sovereign individual' as little as possible, that it should protect his rights at all times, that it should state clearly what was forbidden and the nature of the penalty attached to infringement. When it came to consider violations of the law, it focused not so much upon the offender as upon his offence, as the diagram on page 86 indicates.

If this chart suggests the ripples which succeed each other when a stone has been dropped into a pool, so much the better, because in fact that is what the history of criminology looks like. It begins by focusing upon the individual crime; then upon the individual criminal; after that, as we move into the outer area, it begins to take the offender's immediate circumstances into account, then the influence of society at large, and finally the whole economic and political set-up. At the same time, the diagram is not meant to suggest that one theory disappeared and another took its place – it was far less clear-cut than that – nor that the sequence of the theories was carefully thought out – it was rather a case of individuals

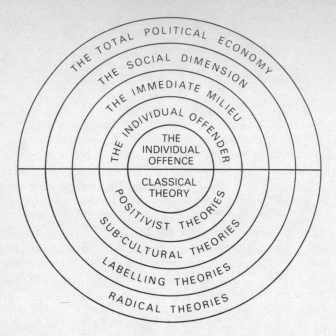

constantly aspiring to a more adequate explanation of crime than those already current. It is only with the benefit of hindsight that the story can be summarised diagrammatically in order to help us on our tour of criminology.

The liberals of the eighteenth century, therefore, concentrated on the criminal act, the distinctions between individual actors, their particular circumstances, etc. being virtually ignored. This was because they regarded each individual as fully responsible for his actions; they would have agreed with W. S. Gilbert's Mikado 'to let the punishment fit the crime'.[4] The punishment should be proportionate to the offence, not varied to suit the personality of the offender; it should be used to deter, but not to reform.

Positivist theories of crime

However, before a hundred years had passed another approach to criminology was in the ascendancy. That is hardly surprising when we remember that the nineteenth century was the century of Charles Darwin, and new theories in the natural sciences; of Auguste Comte and Herbert Spencer, and the beginning of the social sciences; and, a little later, of Sigmund Freud, and the advent of psychiatry and psychology. Attention was now switched from the crime to the criminal: the offender was seen no longer as free and responsible but as one whose behaviour was virtually determined by certain biological, physical or psychological peculiarities; he was different from 'normal' men; he should receive not punishment but therapy. The advocates of this school came to be known as Positivists, because like Comte, who first used the expression 'positivism' in his philosophy, they insisted that what mattered were hard, positive facts, only what falls within the ambit of scientific observation and experimentation.

The founding father of this school, Cesare Lombroso, takes us to the heart of its outlook when he uses the expression 'il reo nato' (the born criminal): a man is a criminal because he is born that way. Lombroso has left an account of what he calls his 'flash of inspiration'. It occurred while he was conducting a post-mortem on the body of a notorious Italian criminal; he noted that the configuration of the skull was not unlike that of lower animals. Then, with a bow in the direction of Charles Darwin, he argued that criminality was a kind of evolution in reverse: the criminal is a 'throwback' to primitive, savage, amoral man; he bears striking physical and mental characteristics to prove it. Further studies brought him to the point where he was able to offer pen-pictures, so to say, of the physical attributes associated with particular crimes: the brilliant eyes and delicate face of the rapist, the cold, glassy eyes, large nose, strong jaws and dark curly hair of the murderer, the mobile hands and face of the thief, and so on.

Although Lombroso's views were comprehensively dismissed by an English prison doctor, Charles Goring, more than seventy years ago,[5] the spirit of Lombroso has continued to haunt the criminological scene. Other attempts have been made to show that the criminal is different from the rest of mankind, that criminality is inherited, that it is linked with particular body structures, or maternal deprivation, or, more recently, with a chromosome anomaly which predisposes to violent, aggressive behaviour. But probably the best-known theory to come from the Lombrosan school in modern times is that propounded by Professor Hans Eysenck.[6]

He argues that an adult's behaviour is decided by what he calls the 'repertoire of conditioned fear reflexes' learned in early childhood. As youngsters, we quickly discover that certain kinds of behaviour have unpleasant consequences, and so, since all of us are utilitarians at heart, loving pleasure and shrinking from pain, we automatically desist from such activity. The significant work in that sentence is 'automatically': true, Eysenck speaks of conscience but he believes that it has nothing to do with conscious choice: it is simply a conditioned reflex, like the salivating of Pavlov's dogs when the dinner bell rang. Not only that, but Eysenck argues that individuals inherit varying degrees of conditionability, so that those who condition easily (the 'introverts' in his classification) become model citizens, providing they receive a reasonable training, whereas those who condition badly or not at all (the 'extraverts') fill our prisons and mental hospitals, no matter how well they are trained in childhood.

Finally, Eysenck suggests that by means of the appropriate drugs an extreme extravert can be moved along the spectrum in the direction of introversion – the criminal can be transformed into the conformist. It is difficult to warm to a theory 'which utilizes a model of human nature where man is a passive actor', and where all moral responsibility is removed from him. In fact, 'there has been a plenitude of critiques of Eysenck from within the ranks of positivism', and 'his research techniques have come under vehement criticism'.[7]

Sub-cultural theories of crime

About the time that Eysenck's theory of criminality appeared, other theories of a more sociological nature were already attracting attention in Britain. (The sociology of crime really began in the early decades of the nineteenth century, when criminal statistics first began to be collated, and the incidence and location and pattern of crime were revealed.) Though the two earlier schools, the Classical and Positivist, differed from each other in many respects, they were at one in focusing their attention on the individual – the individual crime or the individual criminal. But now we come to theories which seek an explanation for crime in the conditions existing within society.

In the decade following the First World War, an important step forward was taken in the sociology of crime with the advent of what has been styled the Chicago school. It grew up around Robert Ezra Park, a reporter turned sociologist, and two of his associates who claimed that Chicago and other large cities consist of a series of zones, rather like the growth rings on a tree trunk, and that crime decreases as one moves from the city centre outwards, until it is virtually non-existent in the high-class bourgeois neighbourhood. So crime is concentrated near the city centre, in the large decaying slum areas which have been vacated by the wealthy as they sought refuge in suburbia. Children brought up in such unpropitious circumstances, where there is so much deprivation and delinquency, 'areas of social disorganisation' as they were euphemistically called, can scarcely escape being contaminated.

One of the great achievements of the Chicago school was that it prepared the way for the series of sub-cultural theories of crime which emerged in America in the late fifties and sixties and quickly spread to the United Kingdom. Lying immediately behind them is the concept, set forth by Robert Merton just before the Second World War, of 'anomie' or lawlessness.[8] His argument is that where you get a whole nation encouraged to pursue certain goals – you have only to think of how the school system and the media, especially advertising, highlight the importance of possessions, of achieving, of getting on in terms of material success – and yet where the legitimate means of attaining those goals is severely limited, then trouble of one kind or another, including crime itself, is bound to result. A British sociologist has illustrated this point by comparing society to a giant fruit machine. But the machine is rigged so that only a select few win consistently. Some play on mindlessly (the conformists), others give up the game in despair (the drop-outs); and others again resort to using foreign coins or magnets to increase their chances of reward (the delinquents).[9] This comparison also helps to explain why sub-cultural theories are often referred to as 'strain theory': the imbalance between the emphasis on material success and the actual opportunities that many people have for such success induces strain, a strain felt most keenly at the bottom of society where opportunities are minimal.

Albert Cohen,[10] the pioneer in this field, notes how working-class boys competing with middle-class boys according to middle-class standards are handicapped from the start: they lack the background and the sophistication. Having failed in school, they find at work that once again they have somehow been sold short, they are not competing on equal terms with many of their peers. And so, frustrated at being always 'at the bottom of the heap', they revenge themselves upon society by uniting with other youths similarly unfortunate and forming with them a 'sub-culture' of their own in opposition to that of society at large; hence the apparently mindless, pointless kinds of delinquency in which they engage, vandalism, for example, or gratuitous violence. It is as though, having had little chance of winning in the middle-class game, they devise their own game in which they do stand a chance of achieving success.

Some criminologists have tried to elaborate on this theory.[11] They argue that youngsters can only make use of the opportunities available to them, and for working-class youngsters even illegitimate opportunities are not evenly distributed. Thus, there is a variety of deviant activities (such as professional crime, violence, addictions and sexual promiscuity) reflecting the different types of opportunities available. However, other criminologists, while continuing to focus on the dynamics at work within the milieu, arrive at conclusions different from those of Albert Cohen.

Walter Miller, for example, maintains that far from being socially maladjusted, working-class youth are only too well adjusted, but to a working-class sub-culture which is itself likely to lead to clashes with the law. Thus, these lads, while not unaware of the opportunities for material success opened up to middle-class boys, are content to pursue what Miller calls 'focal concerns' of their own. These concerns centre upon toughness and smartness, the search for excitement, the desire to be one's own boss, a sense of fatalism, and they easily spill over into delinquent activity.[12]

David Matza rejects both Cohen's idea that crime arises from a delinquent sub-culture fashioned by deprived youngsters and Miller's that the working-class sub-culture itself is more or less conducive to delinquency. He claims that boys tend to drift in and out of crime, so that it is not so much 'a way of life' (as other theories would have us believe) but 'a fact of life', an intermittent activity.[13] In the main they do not reject traditional standards as such, but from time to time resort to rationalisations to justify certain delinquent activities; thus, they might argue that theft is justified because the victim deserved it or could afford it, or because everybody thieves. They are then in a state of 'drift' which can easily result in crime. Moreover, Matza contends, many of the characteristics displayed on the grand scale by delinquents – being tough, taking risks, seeking easy money – are highly valued by all the social classes. They are the 'subterranean values' of the whole of society, though its more fortunate members can pursue them in socially acceptable ways, such as gambling, going to night-clubs, even huntin', shootin' and fishin', not to mention taking vicarious pleasure in the exploits of the young which they read about in Sunday newspapers!

These theories were tried for size, so to say, in Britain and were found to be a less than perfect fit. David Downes recounts in his book *The Delinquent Solution*[14] what he discovered from his research among adolescent East Enders in the London of the early sixties: many of the concepts used by American sociologists hardly seemed to apply. Youngsters had not imbibed at school lofty goals that they could never attain; and similarly, at work, their expectations were realistically pitched at a pretty low level. Why then, he asks, did they get into trouble with the law at all? He seizes upon the word 'boredom', which the youngsters themselves so frequently offered as the reason for much of their delinquency. This word takes on added significance when applied to the domain of leisure, the one domain which they regard as specially their own. They are fatalistic enough about school and work, they have come to realise that their capacity to make things happen their way is negligible, but in leisure they have the chance of expressing their character through action. In fact they often find that the reality of leisure is the counterpart of work – a dreary 'caff', nowhere to go, too little cash for drink, etc. And so in a sort of desperation they turn to crime, either to obtain money to finance the 'high life' they yearn for, or because they see delinquency itself as a means of 'manufacturing' excitement.

Labelling theory of crime

However, in the mid-sixties labelling theory, another American product, began to catch the attention of criminologists. Sub-cultural theorists had argued that it is not enough to take account of the individual offence and the individual offender; consideration must also be given to the wrongdoer's milieu, the small world in which he lives and moves and has his being. Labelling theorists went a step further: attention must be paid to the interactions that take place within the society at large. To put it another way, an eye must be kept not only on the 'actors' (the wrongdoers) but also on the 'audience' (those who react to them).

Howard Becker, one of the leading labelling theorists, shows how some people become marijuana smokers in much the same way as other people become cigarette smokers, but they face an entirely different reaction on the part of the agencies of control.[15]

Labelling theory invites us to face a number of awkward questions. For example: is crime as objective a reality as most of us take it to be? If what is regarded as deviant differs from one country to another, and even within the same country from one time to another, if, for instance, consenting male adult homosexuals are treated as criminals before 1969 but as legally innocent thereafter, does it not look as though deviancy is not necessarily inherent in activities, but rather a label which is attached to them? And if this is so, who does the labelling, and why? Again: how do certain people come to be labelled as criminals, and others who may be involved in similar activities do not? Are not the official records of crime in some degree a reflection of the attitudes of those who enforce the law and of agencies like the mass media which mould public opinion?

Furthermore, the proponents of this school argue, the very measures taken to control some offences may have exactly the opposite result; they may in fact 'amplify' crime because they are an over-reaction: they tend to label people, and then the labelled begin to act in accordance with expectations.

However, perhaps the real value of labelling theory is not as a theory of crime but rather as a highlighting of the factors which help to decide whether this or that person will be labelled delinquent or not. Thus, to take three examples, it draws attention to:

1. The influence of power – the more powerful an individual, the less likelihood there is of his being labelled a criminal (think of Watergate);

2. Social distance – the greater the distance between us and other groups, the easier it is for us to fix labels on them without qualification, to be taken in, if you like, by the stereotype presentation of them in the media (think of the striking miners as portrayed by television);

3. Visibility – the more visible you are the more vulnerable you are; since the police patrol streets and not drawing-rooms, hidden delinquency is scarcely a possibility for those who lack what have been called the 'institutions of privacy' – like dossers, or working-class youngsters from high-rise flats whose only playground is the open street.

Radical theories of crime

By the 1970s a new approach to criminality had emerged. It has been variously described as 'new', 'radical', 'critical' and 'Marxist'. The three British criminologists who launched it – Ian Taylor, Paul Walton and Jock Young[16] – do in fact look at crime from a Marxist perspective. They argue that no previous criminological theories have gone far enough: none has taken into account the whole political economy, or, rather, they have simply taken it for granted. But the real seed ground for crime is the capitalist system itself; with its class conflicts and its exploitations of the proletariat, it is criminogenic. In their socialist Utopia – they never really explain how it will come about – society will be virtually 'crime free', because, on the one hand, the terrible material inequalities of capitalist society, which give rise to crime, will be smoothed away, and, on the other, many of the activities which are currently disapproved or prohibited (usually associated with moral issues like abortion, prostitution, etc.) will be decriminalised.

In view of what we know of socialist states at present in existence – their almost puritanical attitude on such issues as prostitution and pornography and their inability to stamp out crime themselves – one may be forgiven for feeling that that there is a certain unrealism about these radical views. But just as every heresy by definition contains its element of truth, so too the Marxist critique of capitalist society, for all its exaggerations, may still have enough truth in it to jolt our consciences, to make us take a closer look at the capitalist system and to enquire if it is above reproach. It was one of the wisest priests I know who, after a visit to South America, remarked: 'Now I understand why for so many people Marxism seems to be the only way out'.

Looking back over our journey, let us not be surprised if, as was suggested at the outset, we are left with a feeling of disappointment. In part the disappoinment stems from a realisation that until fairly recently the studies of criminologists have tended to concentrate almost exclusively on those sections of the community most heavily represented in prison: on youngsters, therefore, rather than on adults, on the working class rather than on the middle or upper classes, and most surprising of all, since it excludes half of the human race from consideration, on men rather than women. It is a fact that throughout recorded history the level of female crime has always and everywhere been far lower than that of male crime. Many explanations have been offered for the immense disparity in crime rates between men and women – women are not as physically strong as men, or lack the skills necessary for many criminal activities; women are less exposed to temptation; women's offences are more likely to lie hidden in the 'dark figure' of unrecorded crime; some typically female 'delinquency', such as prostitution or lesbianism, is not treated as a criminal offence; women are more law-abiding: it is significant that even in the twenty years between 1962 and 1982, when female crime (as indicated by the number of 'notifiable' offences) increased by a record 138 per cent, the male crime rate rose almost as steeply. Perhaps the most promising explanation of all is that girls and women experience strong social pressures and expectations to behave in non-violent, responsible, law-abiding ways. If further research were to show that this is in fact the case, it might lead us to 'reconsider, as far as it is within our power, the conventional forms of the upbringing and socialization of males';[17] it would also justify our disappointment that criminologists have been accustomed to work within a fairly restricted section of humanity.

However, as we draw towards the end of this survey of the theories of crime, there is another more general reason for disappointment. It is this: that despite all the work of the criminologists, despite all the enlightening information they have to offer, much of it echoing our own experience, the vital touchstone that would finally explain criminal behaviour – even that of young working-class males – remains as elusive as ever. Our own frustration is shared by many of the criminologists, like the one who admitted: 'If only delinquents themselves would disclose their secret, how many years of intellectual toil could be saved?'

It was at the end of an interview with Jimmy Boyle that John Mortimer wrote: 'Crime can't be written off as being just the accident of environment or birth. Perhaps there is something to be said for the Christian doctrine of original sin' (we seem to be back in the garden again). 'But', he added, significantly, 'if you believe that you must also accept the possibility of redemption.'[18] And there, perhaps, is the cue to turn from the criminologists to the theologians.

Christian reflections on crime

There is of course no specifically Christian theory of crime. But there are some traditional Christian insights which have a bearing upon what the criminologists are saying. At times they may call into question the validity of a particular theory, at other times they will provide an additional perspective, and, more often than might be expected, they will be of interest even to those who do not subscribe to the Christian premises or feel easy with Christian terminology. Such notions as freedom, sin, grace and the nature of man ought not to be ignored by those who are concerned with crime – still less by those who have a deep human concern for criminals. Inevitably these notions tend to overlap, but it may be useful to consider briefly each one of them in turn.

Freedom

The gospels tell us that Jesus 'knew what was in man' (Jn 2:25). He understood men and women as no one else ever has, and as part of that understanding simply took for granted in his actions and his teaching the fact of human freedom and responsibility. In our days we are keenly aware that that freedom is not absolute. The psychologists and sociologists have succeeded in showing how deeply it is influenced by a host of other factors – genetic inheritance, for example, social background, family upbringing; in fact, some of them have been so carried away by their success that they now argue that human freedom is non-existent, a figment of the imagination. Such a negative outlook can easily creep into theories about crime: man, and especially criminal man, can be presented as completely determined by biological or psychological or social constraints: 'he's depraved', like the boys in *West Side Story*, 'on account he's deprived'.

But to say that inherited deficiencies or desperate social circumstances encourage crime is not the same thing as saying that they cause it. After following up, over the course of ten years, the careers of 400 randomly selected schoolboys Donald West, a psychiatrist, and David Farrington, a psychologist, were able to report that 'certain adversities are linked with delinquency and ... an accumulation of these adversities makes a delinquent outcome more probable'; they were even able to cite the five background features that seemed most critical – low family income, large family size, parental criminality, low intelligence and poor parental behaviour; but they have to admit in the end that: 'A statistical correlation does not necessarily imply a causal link'. In fact, even those lads they predicted as most vulnerable stood a better than evens chance of not becoming delinquent.[19] As Terence Morris notes: 'prediction is not prophecy';[20] it does not affect the individual's freedom. In fact the criminologist David Matza has coined the expression 'soft determinism', apparently in an attempt to give due recognition to the intensity of the pressures that seem to 'determine' human behaviour, while refusing to deny the central core of freedom in man.

Of course, it is undeniable that some people's freedom of choice *is* badly impaired, but seldom are they 'programmed' to such an extent that they can confidently be adjudged to lack all responsibility for what they do. The rabbi Harold S. Kushner sums up the Judaeo-Christian tradition when he writes: 'To say ... of any criminal that he did not choose to be bad but was a victim of his upbringing, is to make all morality, all discussion of right and wrong, impossible. It leaves unanswered the question of why people in similar circumstances did not all become (criminals). But worse, to say "it is not his fault, he was not free to choose" is to rob a person of his humanity, and reduce him to the level of an animal who is similarly not free to choose between right and wrong'.[21]

Sin

To acknowledge freedom as an integral part of human dignity is also to accept the possibility of wrong decisions being deliberately made, of sin being committed. Sin is a reality in our world, just as it has always been. It is difficult to come close to criminals or be aware of certain types of criminal behaviour without being vividly conscious of the presence of sin: hatred, greed, lust, unforgiveness and, in the most extreme cases, an apparent delight in wickedness for its own sake. Put quite simply, from a

Christian perspective, a sin-free world would be a crime-free, and therefore a prison-free, world. Indeed it is a criminologist of long experience who despairingly concludes that: 'It seems we have rediscovered "sin", in the absence of a better alternative!'.[22]

Yet a Christian sees the recognition of sin not as a counsel of despair but as a ground for hope. This is how it is expressed by a well-known Methodist writer, acquainted with the prison scene and the work of chaplains: 'The view that man is a sinner is the only truly hopeful view of him ... There is certainly no hope for man if the wrongness in human lives is the result of social and hereditary forces beyond human control or is to be explained in terms of psychological sickness. A person can start hoping the moment he stops regarding himself as a victim and sees himself in Christian faith as a sinner. We are, of course, all to some extent victims, and how much we can never know, and this is why ... the believer learns to be very nervous about the risky game of blaming people for their disasters and eventually abandons it. However, in order to live with dignity and self-respect and hope each one of us must believe in that blessed margin of his experience in which he can say "through my fault, my own fault, my own most grievous fault". ... the belief that human responsibility is a reality is part of the gospel'.[23]

To accept man's freedom and his sinfulness does not necessarily lead, however, to the extraordinary attitude towards criminals evinced by those who say: 'Oh, don't worry too much about prisoners. Every person in prison is a volunteer; they put themselves there by what they do'. Not only is such a statement in obvious contradiction with the facts – most prisoners of my acquaintance are much more in the nature of conscripts than volunteers – but it is also a caricature of the Christian viewpoint. Christians, as the quotation in the last paragraph testifies, should be ready to admit that they are in no position to pass final judgement upon another human being or to assess his real guilt. More than that, they remember how bitterly our Lord condemned those who provide what have traditionally been called 'occasions of sin', circumstances which strongly entice others to wrong-doing and give opportunity for it.

Perhaps it was with that in mind that Bishop Sheppard in his powerful Dimbleby Lecture in 1985 contrasted the long list of 'locked doors' which 'make very large numbers of people feel powerless', and the generous prospects facing those who belong to 'comfortable Britain'. In the same vein, the Archbishop of Canterbury had this to say at the AGM of the National Association of Prison Visitors in May 1984: 'While there remains profound division in our society, while people can be seen, and see themselves, as the losers amidst the fortunate majority, there will always be those who seek a short-cut to the life-style they see paraded before them through our advertising and our televisions. We ... would be foolish ... to pretend that there is not a large minority of people who live on the margins of our society and in environments which are themselves a provocation to lawlessness and which provide constant opportunities for it.

'I do not seek to excuse those who offend, for to ascribe purely environmental reasons to every infringement of the law is to deny the individuality and integrity of every human personality. But if we deny to many people the legitimate means to share the fruits of our collective success, we cannot be surprised that they should pursue alternative means to secure what they consider their due.'

Sin lies not only in criminals but also in the law-abiding – and those who have escaped detection; not only in individuals but also in systems and environments. As a French prison chaplain used to say: 'most young delinquents don't begin as delinquents, they begin as society's victims; they are often more sinned against than sinning'.

Grace

The roots of evil are deeper and spread further than we might at first imagine; I find myself agreeing with Canon Douglas Rhymes when he suggests that instead of making a solemn descent upon Soho, which he had described as a square mile of sin, Billy Graham might have been better advised to descend upon Surbiton or Purley.[24] But even the ubiquitous presence of sin need not cause undue alarm, for as Paul assures us: 'where sin abounded, grace abounded all the more' (Rom 5:20). God does not leave us on our own, whether as individuals or as society: his grace, the fruit of the redemptive work of Christ, is at our disposal. We have already had occasion to note that grace builds upon nature, but John Mahoney, SJ, the F. D. Maurice Professor of Moral and Social Theology in London University, warns us against viewing the relationship between them as similar to that of one layer of a wedding cake upon another; rather, he suggests, pursuing the wedding reception simile, it is more like the sherry trifle where the ingredients are inextricably intermingled, where the potency is undoubtedly greater than in the unlaced variety, but where the trifle is every bit as essential to success as is the sherry.[25]

The implications of this are important: God's work in society, as in individuals, is to some extent conditioned by the nature of that society. And so if we wish to understand criminality we need to consider the 'flavour' of society: is it conducive to goodness or evil? is it likely to encourage or oppose the effects of God's grace? This is a point at which criminologist and theologian may not be too far apart. One of the most influential theories in criminology was put forward by Edwin Sutherland. In simple terms, according to his 'theory of differential association',[26] the likelihood of a person's becoming a criminal depends upon whether the influences ('the definitions', in Sutherland's terminology) he encounters in life are on balance for or against lawbreaking: a Fagin's kitchen will, not unexpectedly, produce first-class pickpockets.

The Christian theologian, while rejecting absolute determinism at the level of the individual – no-one *has* to act badly, whatever his circumstances – readily accepts that there are situations of deprivation and inequality which foster criminal activity to a degree that is predictable at the social level: they are criminogenic situations or, to use the kind of language with which he may be more familiar, they are situations which hinder the effectiveness of God's grace in society. When the Prison Chaplains' Association of Pennsylvania produced a car-sticker which read: 'Stop crowding prisons; start crowding churches', their approach may have been somewhat simplistic, but it rightly drew attention to the fact that societies tend to get the criminals they deserve.

The other side of that coin is that where a society is healthy – where moral values are honoured, the family held in high esteem, the Christian heritage respected, all the citizens able to enjoy a reasonable standard of living – the incentives to wrongdoing will be reduced. And those who help to bring about such a society are, whether they realise it or not, helping to promote the coming of God's Kingdom in this world. As John Mahoney argues, just as there are social aspects of sin, so also there are social aspects of grace. 'The grace available to individuals as social beings' he writes, 'must also include grace channelled through other individuals, through groups, through structures and institutions', and when these 'social channels' do admit of being instruments of God's love, then 'they are grace-ful'.[27]

The nature of man

'There is just one small defect in man, the crown of all God's creation', wrote G. K. Chesterton, 'he is not to be trusted.' Yet the very unpredictability of man is, by the kind of paradox which Chesterton himself would have enjoyed, some indication of his mysterious nature and the extent of his greatness. He is unpredictable because he is endowed with a free will; unpredictable because he is capable, both of the depths of evil and the heights of goodness; unpredictable because he can rise above adversities in heredity and background; unpredictable because in addition to the pressures of society he can also be touched by the redemptive grace of God which is not open to scientific investigation; unpredictable because he is always unique.

The psalmist wondered aloud why God, the mighty creator of the universe, should bother himself with puny man, but then rejoiced to recall that 'thou hast made him little less than a God' (Psalm 8:5). It is as though something of the mystery of God is reflected in the nature of man, so that it is not only the sinner but also the saint that is beyond our understanding. We need not be too disappointed that the criminologists have failed in their pursuit of the holy grail – the secret of criminality. Man, even the criminal, is too wonderful, too mysterious a being to be completely understood by anyone except his Maker. The key to his behaviour will always lie beyond us, for he is not like a laboratory specimen that can be 'pinned down' by the psychologist or the sociologist or the psychiatrist, and neatly analysed and explained. He is little less than a god.

But though man may surpass our understanding, the fact remains that at times men and women behave in a way that is harmful to others, they do wrong, they act criminally. What are we to do then, with these creatures little-less-than-a-god? Can we punish them? Dare we punish them? How should we punish them? These are the kinds of questions a prison chaplain has to tussle with; they are the questions we shall be addressing in the next chapter.

8

PUNISH AND BE DAMNED?

All standards of corrective justice are organically related to primitive
vengeance on the one hand and to the ideal of forgiving love on the other.

(Reinhold Niebuhr)

Prisons are above all a moral issue and must remain so.[1]

Each Sunday after divine worship, we – the altar servers, the readers and
myself – would gather in the vestry, to share a cup of coffee and a biscuit,
sometimes a cigarette and usually a fund of jokes. On one occasion I told
them the old story about the little boy who each night would kneel at his
bedside and ask God to bless his father and mother, his grandad and
grandma and himself. One night he made no mention of grandfather,
despite his mother's remonstrances, and the next day the old man died.
However, no one suspected any connection between the two events
until, a few months later, grandmother was omitted from the youngster's
prayer and within twenty-four hours she too was dead. And so when,
after another six months, the boy refused to ask God to bless his father,
there was great consternation. At the end of twenty-four tense hours of
wondering how and when the fatal blow would fall, father arrived home
from work at the point of exhaustion.

'What a day I've had', he murmured to his wife as he staggered
through the front door. 'It's been terrible, I can't remember another like
it.' 'You've had a terrible day?' she replied. 'It couldn't have been any
worse than mine. Do you know what happened to me this morning? The
milkman dropped dead on the back-kitchen floor!'

As the story reached its punch line, there was a great ripple of
laughter, and then, as the laughter subsided, one of the prisoners looked
over at me and grinned. 'I might have guessed it', he commented, 'the
Lord always gets his man!' It was said good-humouredly enough. Yet I
suspect that it was expressing what many people believe deep down: that
God punishes; indeed, since he has eternal punishment in his armoury,

he is the Punisher *par excellence*. And of course once that point is reached, there is no difficulty in arguing – as I once heard a group of Christians argue – that if punishing is good enough for God, then surely it must be good enough for us, too.

But of course this begs the whole question: does God in fact punish at all? For my part, I do not accept that he does. He no more punishes than he walks in the garden of Eden in the cool of the evening or, in the face of human wickedness, regrets that he ever created human beings in the first place. In its references to divine punishments, the Bible is speaking anthropomorphically: it is attributing to God reactions and ways of behaviour which are more appropriate to human beings than to their Maker. It is not God who punishes, but rather it is man who punishes himself: as a moral being, he cannot *do* evil without *becoming* evil. As a free creature, he cannot reject the offer of relationship with God without losing that relationship; and if his rejection is final, then so is his loss – his self-imposed eternal punishment.

All this must not be dismissed as a theological digression. It is a vital reminder that the act of punishing is a peculiarly human phenomenon: it has no divine precedent, nor has it any counterpart in the animal kingdom. Not only is it peculiarly human, it is also very close to the instinctive in man, separated perhaps only by a hair's breadth from the instinctive spirit of revenge. Therefore, it needs watching; perhaps every talk or article about punishment ought to be prefaced by a kind of government health warning: 'Remember, punishing can seriously damage moral health'.

There is, however, a second note of warning that ought to be sounded. Raymond Brown, a scriptural scholar of international repute, has drawn attention to the danger of what he calls 'moral actualism', by which he means taking a leap from a scriptural text to the solution of some current ('actual') highly complex moral issue. The example he gives is of the earnest young Christian who, having spoken at length about our Lord's words in Matthew 25 – 'I was hungry, thirsty, naked, sick, etc. and you did not come to my aid' – suddenly concluded: 'And therefore multi-national companies are clearly immoral'. Maybe, notes Brown, multi-nationals are immoral, maybe they are not, but their moral value certainly cannot be deduced 'neat' from Matthew 25.

It would be unwise and unhelpful, then, to attempt to draw up lists of biblical texts for and against punishment, facing each other like opposing armies, as though the matter could be settled on the basis of which of the two proved to be the stronger. The fact is that the Bible seems simply to accept that punishment for wrongdoing is part and parcel of life in society, and nowhere addresses itself directly to the question of how and whether it can be justified; though of course it asserts that in the social order, and that presumably covers the area of punishment, also, love must express itself in justice. However, that does not mean that the Christian can afford to ignore the Bible, and especially the New

Testament, for, as we shall see, it has its own contribution to make to the punishment debate, 'an ancient and profound debate', as the Archbishop of Canterbury described it in his address to prison visitors.

An ancient and profound debate

Some years ago a book dealing with punishment took as its subtitle: 'Concerning a very old and painful question'.[2] Undoubtedly, a very old question: it has been debated by philosophers and theologians down through the centuries. And certainly a very painful one: if it were not so painfully complex and difficult, it would have been settled long ago.

Few people would disagree with John Locke's common-sense statement: 'We must, wherever we suppose a Law, suppose also some Reward or Punishment attached to that Rule'. But where people do disagree among themselves is in the justification they offer for punishment; and some justification is obviously needed since by definition punishment is unpleasant; it involves the deliberate imposition upon an individual of pain or deprivation.

Punishment as retribution

Until well into the eighteenth century the justification traditionally given was that of Retribution (though it is difficult to believe that the savage penalties imposed were not intended to be horrifically deterrent, too): the moral order had been thrown out of balance and justice demanded that it should be restored by an appropriate measure of punishment; the criminal should receive his just deserts. This notion of retribution is summed up in stone by the statue of Justice perched on the dome of the Old Bailey with a pair of scales in her hands; and it is summed up in theological language by Archbishop Temple when he wrote: 'It is, I believe, the first moral duty of the community, and of the State on its behalf, to re-assert the broken moral law against the offender who has broken it'.[3]

Unfortunately, 'retribution' is often taken to be a thinly disguised excuse for revenge – thus George Bernard Shaw acidly pointed out that though the Bible declares: 'Vengeance is mine, says the Lord', the Lord in question is not the Lord Chancellor! But the aim of retribution is the precise opposite, for it removes from individuals the temptation to exact vengeance by leaving the State to take appropriate action against the wrongdoer. However, because retribution is so easily misunderstood, because of its former association with fierce penalties and, perhaps above all, because of the absence of any moral consensus in Britain about what is right and wrong, retribution has come to be regarded as reactionary, outmoded, at best a protection against lynch law. For almost two hundred years it seems to have been steadily losing ground as a reputable justification for punishment, at least in liberal and intellectual circles. But under a less provocative title it has begun to re-emerge in more recent times, as will be revealed later in this chapter.

Punishment as deterrence

During the late eighteenth century and almost the whole of the nineteenth century, another theory of punishment remained dominant, the theory of Deterrence. (Even today most people would place deterrence very high on their list of justifications for punishment.) Its roots lay in the Utilitarian principle that State activity should be directed towards 'the greatest good of the greatest number'; and one of its staunchest champions was the Italian Beccaria, whom we met in the last chapter. In reaction to the capriciousness and savagery of penalties meted out to wrongdoers in his day, he argued that punishment should be used solely for the protection of society and that, accordingly, it should be reduced to the minimum necessary to deter the criminal from doing further harm to his fellow-men, and to deter others from committing similar offences.

The theory was given wide currency by Jeremy Bentham who, as a Utilitarian philosopher, believed that 'Nature has placed mankind under the governance of two sovereign masters, pain and pleasure'. Therefore, he argued, the surest way of reducing crime and safeguarding society is by ensuring that everyone knows that the gains or pleasures they might derive from wrongdoing would be outweighed by the pain they would suffer by way of punishment. On close inspection the theory seems to be at least a three-pronged affair (though one writer maintains that it could be understood in seven different ways!). It argues that the purpose of punishment is, first, to deter the *individual* from further misbehaviour; second, to deter others from following his example (*general* effect); and, third, to show society's abhorrence for crime and thereby inculcate and reinforce standards (the '*moralising*' effect). In regard to the last point it seems clear that the law with its attendant sanctions builds up patterns of behaviour unconsciously – a person instinctively reaches for his safety-belt once the law has made the wearing of such protective harness compulsory.

It would be foolish to deny the deterrent effects of punishment in any of the senses just indicated, but at the same time it would be naive to imagine that we can assess them with any degree of accuracy. Too many variables have to be taken into account: the nature of the crime (carefully planned or impulsive? against persons or against property?); the type of person involved (one whose only concern is the satisfaction of current needs, or one who postpones present satisfaction for the sake of long-term interests; or, to use the neat terminology of Margery Fry, a 'present dweller' or a 'future dweller'?); the likelihood of being caught and dealt with (sureness and swiftness of punishment are more likely to deter than is mere severity). There is much to be learnt from the fact that when the most appalling penalties were in vogue, even for minor crimes, pickpockets often plied their trade among spectators at the foot of the gallows.

However, if deterrence is empirically difficult to assess, it is also ethically flawed. It does not seem to rule out the use of excessive penalties, such as those currently used in countries like Saudi Arabia, or even the punishment of the innocent, if that would serve the purpose of protecting society or discouraging would-be offenders. The recourse to deterrence as the basic justification for punishment looks like an attempt to make the end justify the means. Indeed, a Christian might argue that the father of Utilitarians was the high priest Caiaphas who said of Jesus: 'It is better that one man die for the sake of all the people' (Jn 11:50).

Punishment as rehabilitation

Broadly speaking, the utilitarian approach to penology may be said to include any theory which finds the justification for punishment not in a past event, the crime committed (as retribution does), but in future events, in the beneficial consequences which, it is believed, will flow from punishment. In this sense, Rehabilitation or reformation can be regarded as a second utilitarian theory of punishment. As we saw in an earlier chapter, the famous Gladstone Report of 1895 unambiguously asserted that 'prison treatment should have as its primary and concurrent objects, deterrence and reform'. Notice the word 'treatment', as well as the word 'reform'. It is the first time in British penal history that prisons have been officially described as places for treatment.

It is a view which remained immensely popular during most of this century, especially in the United States, although, as Professor Anthony Bottoms indicates, 'it is only since the last war that the essentially Christian notion of "reform" became "rehabilitation" – that is, religious and moral impulses in reformation became secularized, psychologized, scientised'.[4] It seems to have much to recommend it. Is there not an air of reasonableness and of humanity about it? Is it not admirably in keeping with Christian aims? Did it not give rise to Rule 1 – 'The purpose of the training and treatment of convicted prisoners shall be to encourage and assist them to lead a good and useful life' – which enshrined a high idealism for the Prison Service? And, besides, what could be better for the individual and for society than that a criminal should be reformed, rehabilitated, made fit for a useful life in society?

With all that I would agree: the ideal is that we should rehabilitate. Unfortunately, however, there are problems. One is that the converging evidence of a number of international surveys indicates that we are not very good at rehabilitating, at least in terms of reducing recidivism;[5] certainly, some people undergo a transformation for the better during a prison sentence, but there is little evidence to suggest that this is the result of the prison regime; nor does one have to be a cynic to suggest that sometimes it is in spite of it. Furthermore, it is simply unbelievable that prison could be the one panacea for all types of criminal activity.

A second problem is highlighted by the way in which the emphasis on reform and rehabilitation has often been linked with the notion of 'curing' people of their evil proclivities. Thus, by the 1950s we were hearing about the 'treatment model' and even the 'medical model' of custody. More and more, crime was coming to be seen as sickness rather than sinfulness; as something to which man is programmed by psychological and sociological factors rather than something for which he is personally responsible. All this threatens to rob him of his human dignity, and also to open up the possibilities of manipulating his behaviour by techniques. I am reminded of the elderly man who had been mugged and left bleeding in the gutter. A first passer-by averted her gaze, a second crossed over to the other side of the road. But a social worker on her way home stopped and gazed down at the recumbent figure and then was heard to murmur: 'How dreadful, whoever did this needs treatment'!

A third problem, following upon the second, is the danger of prolonging sentences beyond that which the crime itself deserves in order that the treatment may be completed: like a hospital patient, the inmate must be kept 'inside' until he is 'cured'. In the United States particularly this led to a growth of indeterminate sentences: prisoners increasingly experienced the dreadful state of uncertainty, as to their time of release, which had been described by Beccaria as 'that cruellest tormentor of the miserable'.

The justice model of punishment

By the early seventies a new model for penal policy was emerging, which was soon to be widely known as the 'Justice Model'.[6] It had far-reaching repercussions for prisoners' rights, for the conditions under which they are imprisoned, etc.

But it also had implications for the understanding of punishment itself. First, the justice model is not primarily concerned with deterring or with reforming, but with 'justice as fairness',[7] with a man's deserts; as Lord Hailsham recalls, even 'a child has a sense of justice (of what is or is not fair) which though unsophisticated and immature is none-the-less as acute and real as the sense of justice of the Lord Chancellor himself'.[8] Second, it looks retrospectively to the crime committed, striving to assess on the one hand the actual harm done and on the other the degree of responsibility of the offender. Third, it allows for 'facilitated change' rather than 'coerced cure';[9] in other words, opportunities for change ought to be provided – otherwise, prison would indeed become a monstrous human warehouse – but ought not to be imposed upon anyone. And, fourth, if it does not positively advocate, the justice model readily accommodates the valuable notion of reparation to the victim of crime.

It seems that, whether intended or not, the justice model is a reinstatement of the apparently discredited theory of retribution. So we have come full circle, and this seems to be the point to pause and take stock. We have looked at three theories of punishment – retribution, deterrence, rehabilitation (and the justice model, which, as I have just suggested, is simply retribution revisited) – and any others would almost certainly fall under one or other of those heads. To some extent the borders are blurred; all of them have something of value to say; and in practice judges and magistrates do not seem to regard themselves as strait-jacketed by any one of them. So, for example, the Lord Chief Justice declared that rape normally calls for a custodial sentence for these reasons: 'First, to mark the gravity of the offence. Second, to emphasise public disapproval. Third, to serve as a warning to others. Fourth, to punish the offender. And last, but by no means least, to protect women'.

However, the question remains: is there in fact one ultimate reason for punishment? and if so, what is it? It is crucial at this point to distinguish between 'reason' in the sense of why we punish (i.e. the *aim*, the purpose, the objective of punishment), and 'reason' in the sense of why it is morally permissible to punish (i.e. the *justification* for punishment). (Obviously, the two do not necessarily coincide: my aim in making constant phone calls to a bookshop is to get them to deliver a book: my justification for annoying them in this way is that I have already paid for the book and I was promised that it would be delivered by yesterday at the latest.) Since punishment involves the deliberate infliction of distress of some sort, there is a *prima facie* moral case against it, and, therefore, the need for an adequate moral justification. But where can such a justification be found except in terms of retribution? As Lord Longford said long ago in his book *The Idea of Punishment*: (Many still believe that retribution is) 'an element in punishment which is essential if punishment is to have any ultimate justification or value. Call this element what you will – retribution or justice or fairness for example. Exaggerate and distort it in one direction or whittle it down in another. Something very deep in human nature nevertheless clings to it'.[10]

It is fascinating, therefore, to find this element surfacing again in the past decade, even if it now appears in the guise of the justice model. If there were no retributive element in punishment would we ever make use of such terms as 'crime' and 'criminal'? C. S. Lewis summed up the situation in his own inimitable fashion in an article he wrote in 1953, and which he had to have published in Australia because it ran so contrary to prevailing views in Britain. ' ... the concept of Desert', he wrote, 'is the only connecting link between punishment and justice. It is only as deserved or undeserved that a sentence can be just or unjust. I do not here contend that the question "Is it deserved?" is the only one we can reasonably ask about punishment. We may very properly ask whether it is likely to deter others and reform the criminal. But neither of these two last questions is a question about justice. There is no sense in talking about a "just deterrent" or a "just cure". We demand of a cure not whether it is just but whether it succeeds. Thus when we cease to consider what the criminal deserves and consider only what will cure him or deter others, we have tacitly removed him from the sphere of justice altogether ... '.[11]

Similarly, Elizabeth Moberly, a Christian in the Eastern Orthodox tradition and the third member of a scholarly family which has taken an intense interest in the question of punishment, insists that 'by asserting that wrongdoers do not *deserve* to suffer, the utilitarians are exposing themselves to the criticism of advocating *un*deserved suffering'. 'By what right', she asks, 'may one deprive a man of his liberty, and subject him (even) to reformative treatment, if this is not deserved?'[12] She admits that utilitarian practice has been better than utilitarian theory, that it has in fact implicitly accepted the notion of desert; and that is surely true.

Whatever particular theory of punishment is espoused, and however valuable the aim of the punishment may be, 'there must be *in addition*', writes Gordon Dunstan, formerly F. D. Maurice Professor of Moral and Social Theology at King's College, London, 'one over-arching moral justification, and that a *sine qua non* of all the others: that is, a principle of just deserts, sometimes called the principle of retribution. Punishment is essentially something to which an offender is obliged to submit because, and only because, of an offence of which he has been found guilty; and the punishment must be proportionate to his guilt; the punishment must fit, not the crime, but his personal culpability. It is this latter clause – that no more may be inflicted upon an offender than his personal culpability warrants – which makes retribution a merciful doctrine, protecting the offender from mere revenge (the vindictive principle); from all forms of social engineering (moulding or breaking the offender into whatever shape society may demand, making it certain that he will be incapable of offending again); and from making him a mere instrument to a social end, the deterrence of others by means of the awful example of what happens to him. I do not say that these utilitarian ends or purposes have no place in a theory of punishment; I do say that they cannot stand there unless governed by the principle of just desert, or of retribution, as I have outlined it.'[13]

Misgivings remain

I suggested earlier that the question of punishment is a painfully difficult one, but I now wish to add that for Christians it is doubly so. To understand Christian misgivings, one need go no further than chapter 6 of St Luke's gospel: 'But I say to you ... Love your enemies, do good to those who hate you ... To him who strikes you on the cheek, offer the other also ... As you wish that men would do to you, do so to them. If you love those who love you, what credit is that to you? For even sinners love those who love them. And if you do good to those who do good to you, what credit is that to you? For even sinners do the same ... But love your enemies ... and your reward will be great and you will be sons of the Most High ... Be merciful, even as your Father is merciful'.

It is against that sort of backcloth that we have to pursue our theological, as opposed to our ethical and philosophical, reflections. Not, as was made clear from the start, that we can expect to make final appeal to any Scriptural text, or series of texts, that will settle the matter once and for all. The Bible is not a book of magical answers to contemporary problems: the best we can hope for, it seems to me, is to reach a conclusion that punishment is not in itself incompatible with gospel morality. (In this respect, the just punishment issue is perhaps rather like the just war issue.)

Yet even this modest hope may seem to be unrealisable when set against our Lord's exacting demands that we should be merciful as our heavenly Father is merciful, and that we should forgive as we ourselves hope for forgiveness. However, mercy must not be misconstrued as permissiveness. A permissive society is merciless: merciless towards the weak and the unprotected. If St Paul, who produced the most magnificent hymn in praise of Christian love – its patience, kindness, etc. – could also regard the authority of the State as coming from God and being used in God's service, not least when it invoked punishments on wrongdoers, may this not be because he realised that a State which provides no measure of security for its citizens against robbery, rape, murder and so on, has failed in one of its most basic responsibilities? There seems to be no avoiding the conclusion that justice and mercy compel us to guarantee social conditions that allow normal people to go about their lawful occasions in peace and freedom.

And what about the Christian virtue of forgiveness? 'A criminal record', said Bishop Harris, 'is, on the surface, a Christian contradiction.' Whether or not we forgive, we certainly find it hard to forget. 'Even more', as the Bishop himself put it, 'we dare not forget.'[14] Some years ago we read in our newspapers of a man who, within hours of his release from prison, with over fifty sexual assaults on his record, had sexually assaulted and murdered the young mother of five children. The crime was tragedy enough, but how much worse it would have been had we learned that he had been released without any reference at all to his record? That would have been utterly irresponsible, and surely a caricature of forgiveness.

In other words, Christian forgiveness is not the same thing as bland benevolence, a sort of mad myopia which refuses to see things as they really are. Furthermore, is it being altogether too pedantic to insist that no one can forgive a wrongdoer except the victim of the wrongdoing? Forgiveness rests in his hands alone. I can forgive the one who has wronged me, but neither I nor anyone else can, strictly speaking, forgive the one who has wronged you.

And yet, when we have offered all our reasonable arguments, are not we Christians still left with the burning question: if the infliction of punishment *is* allowed us by the Lord, may that not be only because of 'the hardness of men's hearts' (Matt 19:8)? The hardness of heart of criminals, clearly enough; their greed, their selfishness, their unconcern for others. In a world where sinful men like these are roaming, the State seems to have no alternative but to protect the law-abiding, if need be, even by punishment. But that 'hardness of heart' is not confined to criminals. Sinfulness, evil, is something which we share in common, a notion strikingly expressed by Alexander Solzhenitsyn. 'If only there were evil people somewhere', he muses, 'insidiously committing evil deeds, and it were necessary only to separate them from the rest of us and destroy them. But the line dividing good and evil cuts through the heart of every human being.'[15]

One of the most frightening things that emerges from the history of punishment is the fact that apparently good men have been so deeply involved in it. The Christian links with the first prison at Cherry Hill in Philadelphia are revealed in many ways, from its very name, 'Penitentiary' (the place where you repent, come to your senses, like the wayward son in the gospel), to the monastic lifestyle imposed upon the convicts. I have suggested that punishment, at least in the form of imprisonment, is permitted because of the hardness of our hearts, because we have not known, cannot think of anything better. Maybe we never shall, at least in the interim period which stretches between the initial coming of the Kingdom in the Christ-event, and its coming in all its perfection in the *Parousia*, when Jesus returns in glory, at the end of time. In its study document, *Punishment and Imprisonment*, a joint working party of the Irish Council of Churches and the Irish Commission for Justice and Peace makes a statement with which many will concur: 'It is our view that prison as punishment is not justifiable in any positive sense in Christian terms. It is tolerable as the least bad alternative only when there is no better way of protecting society'.[16]

To see prison at best as an imperfect structure, which God tolerates rather than something he positively wills, has the enormous advantage of never allowing us to rest content with things as they are. We shall be, or should be, incorrigible reformers. Among those sometimes thought-provoking little stickers with which motorists adorn their cars, one of my favourites reads: 'I used to be complacent, but now, thank God, I'm perfect'. We can never afford to be complacent about our prison system, never be satisfied that at last we have got things even remotely perfect. Indeed, the more we examine the situation, the more we shall become conscious of the pervading effects of sinfulness, in all kinds of ways:

somehow our justice and penal systems seem to be alien to the spirit of love, of justice and of forgiveness which pervades the Gospel. Let me draw attention to just four or five 'black spots', so to say, taken almost at random, which must give us pause for thought.

• Only a tiny percentage of those who commit serious crimes end up in prison, and of course many grave sins, like pride or the cynical destruction of a marriage by adultery, are not crimes at all. It is generally agreed that the 'dark figure' of crime, that is to say, the percentage of crime that goes unrecorded, is substantial. But even of those crimes known to the police, less than half are ever cleared up; and of those, only about one in five results in a sentence of imprisonment. And so Leon Radzinowicz, an international figure in the field of criminology, has estimated that no more than 15 per cent of crime committed is actually punished.[17] This, in turn, means that those who languish in our prisons represent only a fraction of those who break the law. Which might suggest that they serve, in some degree, as the scapegoats for the rest of society?

• Those at the lower end of the socio-economic ladder are grossly over-represented in prison. Yet surely no-one would try to sustain the view that the people who come from social classes IV and V are inherently less virtuous than those who are materially more fortunate. The graffiti writer who responded to the question scrawled on a prison wall: 'Why are 95% of inmates from the working class?' with the words 'Because the working class commit 95% of the crime'[18] may have had a sense of humour. But he had little understanding of the working class, or of the extent of white-collar crime, or of the view, widely held, that justice and penal systems tend to be weighted against certain sections of the community. An article in *New Society*, under the title 'Scandal in the City', reports that fraud may be costing this country over three billion pounds per year, and continues with the comment that most people seem 'to view bank robbers as real criminals and City swindlers as gentlemanly amateurs, even though the bank robbers' hauls are usually small compared with City pickings'.[19]

It is also the case that ethnic minorities are over-represented: in mid-1985, the proportion of prisoners under sentence known to be from ethnic minorities was double their proportion in the comparable age group in the general population.[20]

• St Thomas More has reminded us: 'We have no windows into men's souls'. At best, human justice is a rough and ready affair: we never can be sure of a person's real responsibility. The Church of England working party in its report *Prisons and Prisoners in England Today* carefully distinguishes between legal and moral responsibility. Of the latter it said '...moral responsibility, so far from existing in a fully-fledged sense in every man...is in fact something into which we grow, as a result of our life experiences, and the way in which we are treated by them and encouraged to see ourselves'.[21] Even when an individual is fully responsible for his actions from a moral point of view, that does not mean that others ought not to bear some measure of responsibility for what he has done. Our prisons stand in some measure as an indictment of our whole society and its way of life.

The point was powerfully made by the Bishop of Memphis in a pastoral letter in which he contrasted what he called 'hot' and 'cold' violence. It refers directly of course to the situation in the United States, but it would be naive to imagine that it had no relevance elsewhere. 'We easily recognise and abhor direct, "hot" violence, such as terrorist attacks, bombings of buildings, murders and rapes. It is harder for most of us to get upset about indirect or "cold" violence, which does not seem as spine-chilling, but is so real that from day to day it chips away at our rights. Conscious decisions perpetuating inferior education in poverty areas are cold violence; landlords who, while collecting rents, do nothing about filth and rot in their slum holdings, commit cold violence, discrimination against women, and abandoning the elderly are forms of cold violence. Violence is done in the manipulation of minds, in wasteful misuse of the world's goods, in inadequate wages, in placing private interests over the common good. Cold violence frequently drives men into acts of direct hot violence. Whose sin is it then?'[22]

● There are sometimes grave discrepancies between sentences passed in different courts (at times even in the same courts) for apparently similar crimes. Obviously, it is impossible to assess the gravity of a crime unless all the relevant facts are known, but when in the same week a man found guilty of rape is fined £2,000 and a man found guilty of riding a motorbike without a crash-helmet is sent to prison, we are surely entitled to feel uneasy about our system of justice. And that unease is reinforced when we take account of the fact that Britain sends more people to prison for a longer time than almost any other Western nation.

● Finally, as we have already had occasion to point out, prison seldom reforms but invariably tends to dehumanise; it is a punishment for crime but does nothing to offer restitution to the victims of crime; it puts away the wrongdoers but all too easily stigmatises them for life; it brings hurt to the criminals and also their families but seldom healing; and, perhaps worst of all, it encourages society to believe that it is doing all that needs to be done, thereby blinding us to our responsibilities for the kind of society we have, for the kind of criminals it produces and for the way our prisons are run.

These are just some of the black spots, points at which we become conscious that prisons are, in a sense, ungodly places, a confession of man's inability to cope with the mysterious evil of sin in himself and in others. A Norwegian High Court judge has remarked: 'Our grandparents punished and they did it with a clear conscience. We punish, too, but we do it with a bad conscience'. I would not want to go as far as that, but I certainly want to suggest that whereas our Christian grandparents punished, and seemed to do so with a clear conscience, we punish too but many of us today are far from easy in conscience at what we do, at least where imprisonment is concerned.

The title of this chapter is 'Punish – and be damned'. I do not believe that we shall be damned, in the theological sense of the term, because of the inept ways in which we punish wrongdoers. But I am not at all sure we shall escape altogether the condemnation of a later and more enlightened generation of men and women. They will wonder, perhaps, why in the last quarter of the twentieth century we lacked the wit or the will to find other more constructive forms of punishment, rather in the way that we ourselves wonder how our forebears tolerated the slave trade until the nineteenth century. They may even wonder why we were not working positively for the day when, except in those extreme cases where no other alternative is available, punishment by imprisonment would be as outmoded in our society as is the cane in the classroom.

9

THE PRISONER AND THE CHURCHES

Christ is like a single body which has many parts ... we cannot do without the parts of the body that seem to be weaker; and those parts we think aren't worth much are the ones we treat with greater care ... If one part of the body suffers, all the other parts suffer with it.

(1 Corinthians 12:12, 22–23, 26)

As long as one man is behind bars, I myself am not free.

(Pope John XXIII)

While we look for him among the free, he is a prisoner. While we look for him in glory, he is bleeding on the Cross.

(Carlos A. L. Cristo)[1]

When he invited me to talk to his youth club about my work as a prison chaplain, the parish priest made it clear that the meeting 'might not be without incident'. One or two of the youngsters, he explained, had a father or brother who had done time 'inside' and they might not be too well disposed towards anyone who had connections with the prison system. I was so pleased, however, to have the opportunity of speaking to a group of Christian youngsters about a topic all too often neglected in church circles, that I gladly accepted the invitation – and the challenge that seemed to go with it.

In the event, things turned out very differently from what I – or the parish priest – had expected. Maybe the youth club members whose relatives had tasted prison at first hand were absent that night, or maybe they did not get a chance to express their views, or maybe they had changed their minds. Whatever the reason, I found myself facing an audience that far from inveighing against the nastiness of prison life, wanted to know why it was not a good deal nastier and more brutish; far from showing any sympathy for prisoners, expressed a great deal of hostility towards them – at any rate towards certain kinds of prisoners, such as child molesters.

A thick-set lad, more articulate than the rest, seemed to sum up the mood of the group when he argued that prisoners are the dregs of society and we should not waste too much time on them; far better, he urged, to think of the victims. I agreed that the victims of crime often do not get the consideration and practical help they deserve. 'Nonetheless', I insisted, 'the topic for our discussion tonight is not the victims of crime; it is those who commit crime, or at any rate those who commit crime and get caught for it. Now are you telling me that these prisoners are the most worthless members of society? That they really are the bottom of the barrel?' Yes, came back the reply, as I had expected. 'In that case', I argued, 'don't you think that our Lord might have had prisoners particularly in mind when he said: "Whatever you do to the least of the brethren"? After all, you've just told me that you see prisoners as more or less the lowest form of humanity. So, if they are not "The least of the brethren", who are?'

There was no answer to that question, but it marked a turning point in the discussion that evening. More importantly, it marked the first step in a kind of conversion experience: I was delighted when, a few days later, I received a letter from the group, thanking me for the evening's event and enclosing a small cheque 'for prisoners and their families'.

I recall this incident because for me it is a kind of parable of what I have found in the Christian Churches at large – except that in many cases the conversion process seems scarcely to have begun. What could I say to the prison governor, a self-professed atheist, who told me that, in giving talks to many different types of people, he found that the most vindictive and punitive audiences of all were almost always the Christian ones? It is amazing that in an area where the Scriptures are so clear ('I was in prison ... you visited me ... you did not visit me'), the mind of so many Christians remains confused. More amazing still, when Christians do try to justify their neglect and unconcern in regard to prisons and prisoners, the arguments they frequently use could just as easily be turned against themselves. It is precisely because prisoners seem to be so undeserving of our concern; it is precisely because - unlike the sick, the hungry, the homeless and the naked – the imprisoned do not arouse our instinctive compassion; it is precisely because they have behaved appallingly and are 'getting what they deserve' – it is for these very reasons that they qualify, so to say, as 'the least of the brethren', or, in the beautiful expression of Mother Teresa of Calcutta, as 'Jesus in one of his most distressing disguises'.

In this chapter I want to show, first, how Christians in particular should be able to pierce that disguise ('Behold, the Man'); and then how the effectiveness of actions for the imprisoned is immeasurably strengthened when they are genuinely ecumenical ('That they may be one'); and, finally, I want to return to the point already alluded to: that, so far as the prison ministry is concerned, Christians cannot afford to be merely 'hearers' of the word; they must be 'doers' also ('Not everyone who says "Lord, Lord"').

'Behold, the man' (Jn 19:5)

'Coming to visit the beasts, are you?' It was an officer who made this tasteless remark; he was referring to a group of men, 'rule 43s', who had recently been found guilty of a series of revolting crimes. I was still very new in prison work. His words took me by surprise. They hurt, and stunned, and shocked me. I could not think what to say. I knew I shared his revulsion for the evil done. Equally, I knew that I did not, dared not, share his attitude towards the evil-doers.

It was, however, a decisive moment for me, a moment for absolute honesty with myself. I had to face the question: those beliefs about the dignity of man which I have always subscribed to, are they simply romantic ideals to be mentally indulged in, or are they awe-inspiring truths to be lived by? Now I could see, as never before, that the key to one's dealings with others is the view (or, better, the 'vision') one has of them: if one sees them as just beasts, then there seems no good reason why they should not be treated like beasts. But, if, despite all appearances to the contrary, they are something more, something infinitely more, how then can one dare to ignore the fact?

The opening pages of the Bible set before us two visions: the one of God, the Creator who 'has the whole world in his hand'; the other of men and women, the summit of creation, made in the image and likeness of God (cf. Genesis 1). These two visions are at the heart of the biblical message, and unfold in the succeeding pages. According to the thought patterns of the Middle East at the time the first chapter of Genesis was written, an 'image', or statue, was something more than a bare reminder of the one it represented: it somehow embodied an active presence; God could be discovered *in* his image. Such is the intimate relationship between God and humankind that the Bible sees men and women as possessing a precious dignity and value; there is in them and in all their fellows (as in so many 'images') the presence of the Creator himself. They are the creatures most like to the living God – the closeness is emphasised by God's decision to make them not only 'in our own image' but also 'in the likeness of ourselves' – they are unique throughout the whole of creation, capable of knowing and entering into a relationship of love with their Maker.

But this initial dignity, stemming from creation, is still further enhanced by the redemptive work of Jesus Christ; human beings have been 're-created' as adopted children of God, and invited to find their eternal happiness in intimate union with their Maker. 'Think of the love that the Father has lavished on us', cries out St John, 'by letting us be called God's children; and that is what we are ... we are already the children of God but what we are to be in the future has not yet been revealed; all we know is, that when it is revealed we shall be like him because we shall see him as he really is' (1 Jn 3:1–2).

The Christian vision, therefore, is that every human being without exception – whether good or bad, intelligent or ignorant, useful or 'useless' – is a being with a unique dignity that nothing can take away: each man and woman is created by God, redeemed by Christ, fashioned to be a son or daughter of God, summoned to eternal glory. I believe that this vision is the most vital contribution which the Christian Churches can bring to the prison world, for it is a vision which bathes that sombre world in a new light and gives it fresh meaning.

But I also believe that it should serve as the most potent stimulus to Christian involvement in the prison ministry, for how can Christian people acknowledge men and women in prison as 'brothers and sisters for whom Christ died' (1 Cor 8:11) and yet, like the priest and the Levite in the parable of the good Samaritan, 'pass them by on the other side' (Lk 10:31, 32)? They have a vision which should enable them both to see much more in every man than the circumstances might seem to warrant, and also to cherish a genuine hope that no human being is beyond conversion and renewal. The two points have been clearly made by an Anglican Archbishop and a Roman Catholic Cardinal, respectively. The first wrote: 'he (the prisoner) is never only a criminal and nothing else ... it is good to think more of what the man may become than of what he is ... to treat the character as what it may be is to treat it as what in actuality it is, for it is chiefly potentiality'.[2] The second ecclesiastic reminded a conference of Italian prison chaplains: 'To believe, despite everything, in the rehabilitation of man, in the salvation of the sinner, is a way of believing in Jesus himself. ... To treat the sinner as a man, whatever his crime, to treat him as a brother, is a capacity which is derived from the power of the gospel'.[3]

It is in the light of the Christian vision that the Vatican Council called for 'reverence for man'.[4] The reverence is most demanded when man appears least deserving of it, and so runs the greatest risk of being treated as something less than he really is. When, for example, he has behaved abominably, especially to the elderly and the weak; when he has forfeited his place in society; when his world has been reduced to the size of a prison cell; when he has lost all belief in himself, and in his value and worth; when he has been handed over to others and is at their mercy.

A colleague who served for several years as the chaplain to a prison for young offenders, many of whom were serving life sentences for murder or other heinous offences, recalled that there were three occasions when his belief in man was put to a terrifying test. On one of them, he was visiting a young chap who together with his companion had tortured an old woman to death in circumstances so brutal and humiliating as to be beyond comprehension. Yet he seemed to be completely impervious to the enormity of his crime. When the chaplain made some reference to it, he simply shrugged his shoulders and said: 'Ah well, why bother about that – it's past history now'. My friend admitted that he had had to leave the cell so that he could go away and weep. I wonder if part of the reason for his tears was that he found it so difficult to discern in that hardened young man the image of God? It is a scholar, very knowledgeable about life in prison and deeply committed as a Christian, who points out that: 'Belief in the essential dignity of Man is as much an act of faith as belief in the existence of God'.[5]

In chapter 19 of St John's gospel, our Lord, having undergone a vicious flogging, is paraded before the crowds assembled in the courtyard of Pontius Pilate's palace. On his head there is a crown of thorns, on his shoulders a purple robe. 'Behold the man', declares Pilate, but, as is so often the case in the fourth gospel, the words carry a hidden depth of meaning for the believer. Superficially this tortured, bleeding Prisoner seems scarcely human; he has become, in the Bible's phrase, 'a worm and no man' (Psalm 22:6); but, to the eye of faith, he is THE Man. Throughout the ages, Christians have knelt in spirit before him, have seen through all the contradictory evidence and recognised him as the perfect Man, and, still more, the unique Son of God. Perhaps, therefore, they can be expected, upon entering a prison cell, to see more in this sorry figure than just a prisoner; still less, just a murderer, or a robber, or a rapist, or an arsonist. 'Behold, the man' – he is a man; made in the image of God, however much the likeness has been distorted; a brother of Jesus, redeemed at the cost of his life's blood; called, just as certainly as themselves or his victim, to an eternal destiny.

To hold on to the Christian vision of man within a prison context may seem to be asking a great deal, but, for myself and so many of those I know, to persevere in prison work without such a vision would be asking the impossible.

'That they may be one' (Jn 17:21)

Almost exactly a hundred years before I made my debut there, Walton prison, Liverpool, had received its first full-time Roman Catholic Chaplain, James Nugent. At his death, in 1906, a statue was erected to his memory, recording that Monsignor Nugent had been 'Consoler of the Prisoner, Reformer of the Criminal, Saviour of Fallen Women' and so on. It was the Borough Act of 1863 which had made it possible for a full-time Catholic prison chaplain to be employed and paid. Or so it seemed. In fact, when the Town Council got wind of the appointment, they, aided and abetted by the Archdeacon of Liverpool, declared that they were not prepared to pay a papist's salary out of the rates. The ensuing controversy was finally settled by the Home Secretary of the day when he ruled that Nugent's earnings would be made up from fines collected at the courts.

That historical cameo is a stark and uncomfortable reminder of the bigotry and prejudice which once divided Christians from one another. Of course, the bigotry was not confined to a particular Church and inevitably it affected the prison scene just as it affected, and infected, every other area of society.

By the time of my entrance into the Service older colleagues were assuring me that I would find a greater degree of ecumenical spirit in prison that ever I had 'outside'. To some extent they were right. Yet the ecumenism I encountered was often superficial and seemed almost accidental. A group of different ministers of religion had been thrown together, literally under the same roof; was there much point in each ploughing his own furrow in isolation? Would there not be sense in combining forces, in view of the fact that they worked in a world, often apathetic and sometimes openly hostile to anything Christian? And, anyway, as they came to know each other at first hand, was there not often a mutual discovery: that they were all rather decent fellows, after all – at least if you managed to get beneath the denominational tags?

However, the next twenty years were to witness a striking advance in ecumenical relationships between the Christian Churches, an advance which was to have its impact upon prison ministry also. At the National Pastoral Congress of the Catholic Church, held in Liverpool in 1980, prolonged applause greeted this statement: 'We give thanks to God for the marvellous progress towards Christian unity which has taken place during the past fifteen years'. There are few chaplains who would not wish to make that statement their own: to give thanks to God for the marvellous ecumenical progress which has occurred in our prisons during the past two decades. The concept of team ministry has begun to 'take' among chaplains, ecumenical co-operation has become declared policy, and ecumenical activity is no longer something which simply shoots up of its own accord, like weeds in the back garden, but rather something we are committed to cultivating, like a prize rose.

It was in the early seventies that an official notice was sent to every penal establishment, stating that the ministers of the different Churches 'are colleagues with no relationship of superiority or inferiority'. And a few years later the decision was made that, 'in view of deepening ecumenical relationships', the title of chaplain, which had formerly been used exclusively of chaplains of the Established Church, should now be extended (with the appropriate prefix of Roman Catholic or Methodist) to other Christian ministers too. These were scarcely earth-shattering events, but for those able to read the signs of the times they were significant, indicating a growing awareness of each other's feelings and a readiness to compromise in order to achieve a closer partnership. They were followed by the joint letter, signed by senior chaplains of all the major Christian bodies, which was sent out in 1977 to prison chaplains, and which, according to one senior official of the Prison Department, may well prove to be 'a watershed in the development of the prison chaplaincy and its work'.

The letter quoted Bishop Ramsey: 'The whole ecumenical enterprise is of the Holy Spirit who is the Spirit of Truth and the Spirit of love, working within us, uniting us in love and building us up in truth ... We must avoid binding the Spirit by our stupidity and narrowness and lack of faith'. It continued: 'In this ecumenical enterprise we are all being called upon to ... try out new approaches without abandoning our integrity, and to take risks for the sake of the gospel. Already within the Prison Department developments have been encouraging – some would even say, exhilarating! For years we have trained together, prayed together and conferred together; friendships are deep and permanent and mutual trust and commitment are growing. Now perhaps is the time to take a new initiative. (And so) we (the senior chaplains of all denominations) ... enter with joy and enthusiasm into a commitment of ecumenical team co-operation'.

The letter insists that a team ministry is valid only in the measure that it can be embodied in ways that are acceptable to all, and it lists 'some faltering steps' in that direction which might be explored. Among them the following:

1. Regular meetings, say every three months, of the whole chaplaincy team, to pray together and to plan their programme together, with the chairmanship of the group being decided as the members think best;
2. arranging programmes of religious education and other similar meetings on an ecumenical basis;
3. sharing out the work load of daily statutory duties;
4. helping to provide emergency cover for absences of one another;
5. extending the practice of ecumenical worship.

The letter ends with a reminder that the whole concept of team ministry and its translation into action are in fact the expression of 'our desire to do nothing separate which may be done together'.

The spirit of openness and mutual trust and readiness for adventure for the sake of the gospel which characterises the 1977 letter has been reflected to a greater or lesser extent in establishments up and down the country. Each year the Prison Department publishes an official report which is a kind of window onto its activities and achievements and aspirations. Here are a few excerpts from some of the more recent reports.

'The manner in which all our ... clergy' (it is a governor reporting) 'co-operate with each other is the finest advertisement for the ecumenical movement that it is possible to devise. We are grateful to them all.'[6] 'The effectiveness of ministry at all levels owes much to the increasing determination of Chaplains to work together as a team and to cross boundaries where risk is justified.'[7] 'Ecumenical relationships between Chaplains have been further deepened during the year by experiments and explorations in crossing boundaries. The visitation of cells, punishment wings, and hospitals as well as the interviewing of receptions are now planned as team activities and in several establishments Chaplains are covering for one another during time off duty.'[8]

However, the record of what has been achieved is to be found not only in the pages of reports but also in bricks and mortar. At one time each penal establishment had at least two chapels, sometimes more. Today, in all but a handful of cases, our prisons have a single chapel shared by all Christians. In some places there is a shared chaplaincy centre which includes not only a chapel but also offices and rooms suitable for various religious activities such as discussion groups, religious drama, films and filmstrips.

It was that revered ecumenical figure, Cardinal Bea, who said that 'The door to unity is entered upon our knees'. One of the most promising aspects of team ministry has been the increasing amount of time that chaplains of all denominations have spent in prayer together. In one of our major prisons the chaplaincy team meet every weekday, say the Divine Office together and pray by name for all the institutions and all the chaplains in a particular part of the country. One of the most memorable prison events I have participated in recently was an ecumenical Good Friday Service, which received the full approval of all the Church authorities concerned. The Liturgy of the Passion, with minor adjustments, was the order of service, and at Communion time the prisoners approached the altar to receive the Sacrament from the appropriate chaplain. There was an enormous sense of oneness as we celebrated together the sufferings and death of our common Lord.

For many years now full-time chaplains have taken part in an ecumenical retreat. It was during one of them that Archbishop Coggan was due to meet Pope John XXIII in Rome and that morning at the Roman Catholic Mass, attended by a number of Anglicans, the celebrant told his congregation, much to their amusement: 'This Mass is being offered for God's blessing upon a very important meeting: today, as you know, the Archbishop of Canterbury is paying a visit to his suffragan in the Vatican!' We have learned not only to pray together, but even to laugh together in our prayers, and that must be a good sign.

It was the growth in ecumenism that made possible the novel and, so far as can be judged, successful series of ecumenical 'Contact' fortnights held in 1984, 1985 and 1986. During a period of two weeks, one on either side of Whit Sunday the great feast of the Holy Spirit, chaplains of all the Christian denominations aimed to visit, to make contact with, every imprisoned man, woman and youngster in the prison system. In the first year, each inmate was offered a card, carrying a message of concern and encouragement from the Anglican, Catholic and Methodist Church leaders. That initial contact was followed up in the second year with the distribution to prisoners of a strikingly designed copy of St Luke's gospel. In 1986, Contact fortnight was centred upon prayer – the response to

God's word – and an attractive card, with a word of encouragement to pray and a brief explanation of how to pray, was taken to every cell in the country.

Of course, visiting cells and personal contact with prisoners are at the heart of the chaplains' pastoral work. But what was special about the Contact fortnights was that an attempt was made to reach out to all prisoners simultaneously in the course of just fourteen days, that it was an ecumenical venture throughout, and that it was supported by a great chorus of prayer from the Christian community outside.

It is not easy to assess what impact ecumenism has had on prisoners themselves, but there seems little doubt that it has made them more aware of all that Christians hold in common, sometimes has left them impatient for an end to disunity, and has given them a more sympathetic understanding of brother – and sister – Christians. At times it has broadened their outlook in unexpected ways; for instance, one Remembrance Sunday, when a combined memorial service for the dead of the two World Wars was being held in a Catholic prison chapel, the Anglican Chaplain invited one of his congregation, a UDA man, to attend. Not surprisingly, the UDA prisoner showed a marked reluctance to accept such a 'dubious' invitation. However, in the end he decided that though he had never set foot in a Catholic Church before he would do so on this occasion. Later, he was reporting with amazement what a revelation it had been: fancy, the Catholics had a Union Jack in their chapel, and, fancy, they read from the Bible, and, fancy, they sang hymns, and some of them good Protestant hymns at that! By any standards, that ecumenical service was not unsuccessful.

An Anglican chaplain was once asked by a Catholic prisoner if he would say some prayers with him. He gently explained that he was a Church of England priest, only to receive the stunning reply: 'Oh, don't worry, Chaplain; any old prayer will do!' Hardly the most felicitous of expressions, yet surely the young man concerned was saying in his own rather gauche way that he had got the ecumenical message – and was fully in agreement with it.

However, the practical working out of ecumenism in prison has not been all sweetness and light. There have been, and still are at times, tensions and misunderstandings and disagreements. There are uncertainties. There are questions to be asked and answered: we have taken risks; have we taken too many, or too few? where do we go, where can we go, from here in the way of ecumenical co-operation? should we be aiming at a Christian rather than a denominational presence? prisoners tend to be traditionalists: are we succeeding only in confusing them? But I believe that one of the most important questions of all concerns the Churches outside: why is it that they have shown so little enthusiasm for joint action in regard to prisons and prisoners? This would seem to be – it certainly should be – an area of common Christian concern: why have they been so shy to speak and act together?

But despite the difficulties and the unanswered questions, we know we have much to thank God for. In the words of Pope John Paul II, we know that we dare not go back on the way we have come nor have we any desire to do so.

I began this section by referring to Monsignor Nugent. If today the reader were to go to Liverpool and pay a visit to St John's Gardens in the city centre, he would find the statue of James Nugent in all its spendour. But that is not all: he would see, facing it on the other side of the Park, another statue, that of Canon Major Lester, an Anglican parish priest, who like Nugent worked heroically for the poor and distressed. To the scandal of many of their co-religionists, they had been firm friends and collaborators for many a long year, and in old age would sometimes be seen walking together through the city arm in arm. It is fascinating that those two good men, though they had never heard of ecumenism, were in their own way among the pioneers of what is happening in the Churches and in so many of our prisons today.

Their story, like the story unfolded in these last few pages, is a particularly precious one, for surely it has a mysterious link with the prayer which was prayed by a young Galilean, as he sat and supped with his friends, on a Thursday evening long, long ago: 'Father', he said, 'I pray that they may be one, as thou, Father, in me and I in thee: I pray that they may be one in us that the world' – and not least perhaps the prison world – 'may know that thou hast sent me' (Jn 17:21–23).

'Not everyone who says "Lord, Lord" ... ' (Matt 7:21)

During the papal visit to Britain, a borstal chaplain returned to his parish overjoyed with the news he was about to share with his people: he had just been given permission by the governor to take six borstal boys with him to one of the sites where the Pope was to celebrate Mass and deliver a major address. The people listened with a notable lack of enthusiasm, and then one of them enquired anxiously: 'Those lads won't be coming with us in our bus, will they? I mean, it wouldn't be safe, would it?' The chaplain looked at his parishioners with mixed feelings of anger and sadness. 'No', he said, 'don't worry; they won't be on *your* bus; the lads and I will make our own way there.' And they did.

It was, I think, a Belgian writer who used the bold expression 'racisme pénitentiaire' to express the prevailing attitude in society towards prisoners; it is a mixture of prejudice and ignorance and fear; it is a conviction, usually unspoken, that prisoners are second-class citizens, that they should be left to make out as best they can in their penal ghettoes; this attitude is a gullible acceptance of the sensational half-truths served up by certain sections of the press and a readiness to believe the worst about prisoners; it is, like racism in the ordinary sense of the word, more pervasive and more deeply embedded than might appear.

Sadly, this attitude is widespread among Christians, too. I have already pointed out that Church audiences are sometimes distinguished by the excessively punitive stance they adopt towards law-breakers. Even worse is the general apathy and indifference Christians display towards prisoners: they simply don't want to know; they would rather not get too involved. It is as though they were re-echoing the querulous complaint of Cain: 'Am I my brother's keeper?' (Gen 4:9). Cain may have thought he was posing a simply rhetorical question – and perhaps many Christians think the same – but in fact the question has an answer. We evade it at our peril. Yes, we are our brother's keepers. Like all our fellow citizens, we are responsible for the prisons of our land; what is done in them is done in our name, on our behalf. As Christians, we should feel the responsibility even more keenly, because, if we take the New Testament seriously, we must recognise that we are not simply our (prison) brothers' keepers: we are their brothers, and 'whatever we do, or fail to do, for the least of the brothers ... '. What an awkward text that is! Father Jon Sobrino, one of the major theologians of 'liberation theology', maintains that the reason why there is so much argument about that type of theology is because it poses a question for us: '"What have we done with our brothers?" (And) ... that is raising the question of God and ourselves – what sort of human beings are we?'[9] Prisons may not give rise to quite so much debate as does liberation theology, but they do, I suggest, give rise to similar questions.

The National Association for the Care and Resettlement of Offenders (NACRO) has earned itself immense respect for its practical efforts to reduce crime, its concern for prisoners and their families and its dissemination of up-to-date information about the justice system. At the end of a lecture she gave a few months ago, its director was asked what support NACRO received from the Established Church. It was clearly an embarrassing moment. She hesitated and then responded: 'Very little'. She went on to say how much the Association would welcome Church support. It was specifically the Established Church that was referred to in the question, but I have little doubt that the answer would have been much the same whichever Christian Church had been mentioned by name. Presumably, that is why at its most recent congress in 1985, the (Catholic) International Commission of Principal Prison Chaplains found it necessary to draw up a 'Message' in which, among other things, it appealed to Church leaders to recognise that the prison ministry is not a marginal task, an 'extra', but a unique and essential apostolate in the Church.[10]

A fascinating 'discovery' has been made in recent years by French chaplains as they reflected, at various regional and national meetings, on the theology of the prison ministry. They began, as they admit, by regarding the ministry primarily in terms of the chaplain, so that other Christian men and women engaged in similar work were seen as *his* partners: they were there not so much of right but rather as helpers of the chaplain. However, little by little, the chaplains were drawn – or 'driven by the Spirit'? – to a rather different understanding: the ministry to the imprisoned is an essential part of the mission of the Church. But the mission of the Church does not rest solely, or even primarily, with the clergy; it belongs to all the baptised. Indeed, the new Roman Catholic Code of Canon Law states expressly that 'they (the faithful) participate in their own way in the priestly, prophetic and kingly office of Christ' (canon 204 §1)[11] – that three-fold office which, as we saw in chapter 6, lies at the heart of the chaplain's ministry. And so, the French chaplains argue, it might be better to speak not of the 'chaplaincy', with its inevitable emphasis on the ordained minister, but rather of the Church's 'pastoral service in prison', a title more suggestive of the universal nature of the prison ministry: the laity are there, not simply helping the chaplains, but carrying out their God-given task as baptised Christians. If all this is good news to many men and women already deeply committed to the prison apostolate, it is, I fear, challenging and even frightening news to very many more who are not accustomed to viewing prisoners as any particular concern of theirs.

I recall at least one occasion when the very failure of some Christians towards prisoners stimulated the conscience of others in a quite remarkable way. A prison chaplain found himself having to explain to parishioners on a new housing estate that he would not be able to celebrate Mass for them on Sunday morning at 9.00 a.m., which was what most of them were hoping for, because at that time he celebrated Mass in the prison and in the prison a service at any other time was virtually impossible. His explanation seemed unconvincing to many of them, who complained that they did not see why regular Church-goers should be put out simply for the sake of a handful of prisoners – who probably never went to Mass outside, anyway. A heated exchange continued along these lines for some time, until eventually a woman stood up and stated that she felt unable to agree with what was being said; to her it seemed to be in conflict with the demands of the gospel.

But that was not all. She urged that the parishioners should not only forgo Mass at the time of their choice for the sake of the prisoners, but that they should as a parish try and do something positive to help their 'fellow parishioners' in prison. Her proposal ultimately bore fruit in a scheme whereby a number of families from the parish volunteered to open their homes to wives and children who had a long way to travel in order to visit their husbands and fathers in prison. The volunteers met the prisoners' families at the station on Friday night, took them shopping in the nearby town next morning, ensured that they reached the prison in good time for their visits on Saturday and Sunday, and finally accompanied them to the station for their return journey.

This splendid scheme, which over the course of several years came to the aid of a number of families who might otherwise have been unable to enjoy visits to their loved ones in prison, assures us that there are

Christians only too anxious to help prisoners and to become involved in the prison ministry. Indeed, in larger prisons, in addition to the normal chaplaincy complement of an Anglican, Roman Catholic and Methodist, there are often other full-time Church appointments, such as personnel from the Church Army or members of religious orders. Moreover, there are many lay men and women who assist the chaplains as official 'voluntary helpers': they run Bible study groups, give Christian instruction, visit individuals, assist at services perhaps by playing a guitar or simply as part of the congregation. Others care for prisoners' families: for example, the Catholic Social Service for Prisoners arranges an annual holiday for prisoners' wives and families in the south-east who would otherwise be unable to take a break, and the Church of England Mothers' Union also offers help to the dependants of those in prison. Some Christians take selected homeless ex-prisoners into their own homes, and one woman, disabled from birth with a progressively crippling disease, has joined forces with a former prisoner, who was converted during his sentence, to provide a Christian magazine for prisoners. In 1958 the Langley House Trust was set up which, while respecting the religious convictions of each individual, took as its principal aim: 'the spreading and sustaining of Christianity among men and women who are ex-offenders ... '. Today it has thirteen homes, three of them catering for elderly men, four serving as half-way houses and four providing sheltered working communities.

Finally, there are those who support the whole prison apostolate with their prayers. For many years the Church of England has run the national Guild of St Leonard to ensure widespread prayer for prisoners and those who work in prison. Individual chaplains or chaplaincy teams often send out circulars on a regular basis to people in the local community who have promised to pray for them and their work, drawing attention, by first names only, to particular inmates who have special needs: 'for John who has recently been brought to faith in Christ, that he may persevere despite his many failures in the past', 'for Mary that she may be reconciled with her family' and so on. Prison Fellowship has also set up prayer-groups for virtually every prison in England and Wales. More recently all the Carmelite convents were approached for prayers; their response and enthusiasm surpassed our expectations, and have been a source of great encouragement. 'As you're stomping round the wings from cell to cell', wrote one chaplain, 'it's good to know there are Carmelites in many places who are accompanying you with their prayer and concern.'

However, though many individual Christians are deeply involved in prison ministry, many more could and should be. And so too, should the Churches. In their statement on 'the Reform of the Correctional Institutions', the Roman Catholic hierarchy in the United States insisted that 'In our response to the urging of Jesus, recorded in St Matthew's gospel, to "visit" those in prisons, it is necessary that we not only visit individuals confined in prison but "visit" the correctional system itself'.[12] I find it hard to believe that the Churches in this country have yet 'visited' the penal system as frequently or as effectively as they might. Such issues as prison overcrowding, prisoners' rights, alternatives to custodial sentences, care of the victims of crime, the uneven incidence of prison sentences in favour of the middle and upper classes, the need to give prisoners greater opportunities for making reparation to those they have injured: all these ought to be at the heart of the Churches' constant concern.

Again, the Churches have a powerful role to play in the prevention of crime, and to prevent crime is to save many people from a great deal of suffering. As a recent report put it: 'The Christian community must ask itself whether it has done enough in schools and especially in homes to provide adequate moral formation for children and young people. Have Christians promoted ... a deep respect for the laws of the land? Have Christians taught their children, especially by way of example, that good citizenship flows out of respect for others and from living the Gospel?'[13] The crucial importance of the Churches' efforts to prevent crime is highlighted by these words of the Lord Chief Justice, in a House of Lords debate in 1982: 'Neither police nor courts nor prison can solve the problem of the rising crime rate. By the time that the criminal falls into the hands of the police, and more particularly by the time he reaches the court, it is too late. The damage has been done. The remedy, if it can be found, must be sought a great deal earlier'.[14]

In its report in 1985, the Archbishop of Canterbury's Commission on Urban Priority Areas devotes its final chapter to 'Order and Law' and emphasises the importance of community-based projects for the prevention of crime, adding: 'We believe that Churches in every locality should help with such initiatives wherever they are appropriate and necessary'. It pays tribute to the contributions that Church members in partnership with others have made to the establishment of victim support schemes and to the provision of volunteers to run them; it acknowledges also other initiatives taken by the Churches, such as the sponsoring of law centres to meet the legal needs of the more disadvantaged members of the community, and the initiating of projects for reparation, conciliation and mediation as the means of settling 'minor' conflicts speedily and without recourse to the courts. Nowhere, however, in the Report is there any assurance that the Churches are doing all that they could or should be doing within local communities; indeed the subtitle of the Report, 'A Call for Action by Church and Nation', would seem to suggest the opposite.[15]

Perhaps the role of the Christian Church in regard to prisons and prisoners could be described as four-fold. First of all, that of constantly reminding the nation, and in particular its own members, of that 'Christian vision' of man and woman outlined in the first part of this chapter, and of the practical consequences that flow from it, both for attitudes towards and treatment of prisoners. It seems that the Churches have let slip a perfect opportunity for doing that by their failure so far to support Prisoners Week as enthusiastically as they might; that week should be the occasion in the year when they are united in presenting a Christian view of prisoners and our duties towards them.

Secondly, there is the task of providing a sufficient number of suitable chaplains to meet the needs of the imprisoned; prisoners cannot come to the Church and, therefore, the Church in the person of the prison chaplains must go to them. It is reassuring to find that an increasing number of theological students are finding placements in prison as part of their training and so are becoming acquainted at first hand with an important ministry which might so easily be forgotten.

Thirdly, the Church ought to encourage Christian men and women to become involved in the judicial system and in work for prisoners. They might undertake such work on a professional basis as prison officers, or prison governors, or probation officers, or judges or police officers. They might devote some of their leisure time to voluntary work: as prison visitors, for example, or chaplains' assistants, or members of organisations concerned with penal affairs, or partners in the kind of local projects referred to a little earlier in this section. They might simply look for opportunities to be good neighbours to an ex-offender or to a prisoner's family.

Finally, the Church ought to summon its people to regular prayer for those who make laws in our country, those who administer them, those who strive to reach a better understanding of crime in all its complexity, and those who suffer because of crime – the victims, obviously, but also the perpetrators and their families.

In the past decade both the Church of England and the Roman Catholic Churches have produced valuable reports on prisons and prisoners,[16] so too has a joint working party representing the Irish Council of Churches;[17] and the Methodist secretary of the British Council of Churches' Penal Policy Group has written a book on the same topic.[18] The Christian point of view has been well represented in word, yet many of us involved in prisons feel disappointed that it appears to have made so little impact even upon Christians themselves. The ideal has not yet been translated into Christian action. Perhaps this is because, as Adrian Speller suggests, Christians are members of society and introduce into the Church many of Society's negative, 'imprisoning' ideas and attitudes towards prisons and prisoners and the whole justice system. Hence the need, as the title of his book indicates, for a 'Breaking Out'.[19] In any event, the sad fact is that we still have not realised the expectation expressed in one of those reports just referred to. 'The apostolate to prisoners', says *A Time for Justice*, 'should not be left to the ministry of prison chaplains and those lay people, all too few, currently involved in the work ... The whole diocese, from the Bishop to children in the schools, needs to be involved in one way or another.'[20] It seems unlikely that such involvement will be achieved until many more Christians are able to identify with their brothers and sisters in prison to the extent implied by the author of the Letter to the Hebrews, when he urges his readers: 'Keep in mind those who are in prison as though you were in prison with them' (Heb 13:3). The invitation to the Churches – and that means all Christians – to find and minister to Christ in the person of the prisoner is not only a privilege; it is also, and always, a massive challenge. For it is inescapably linked with another demand, the demand for conversion, for newness of vision and for a change of heart, which may well go against the grain and prove extremely costly. But then the gospels have never suggested that it would be anything but costly to advance from saying 'Lord, Lord' to doing the will of the Father in heaven.

10

LESSONS I HAVE LEARNED 'INSIDE'

We need heralds of the Gospel who are experts in humanity, who have penetrated the depths of the human heart, who have shared to the full the joys and hopes, the anguish and the sadness of our day, but who are, at the same time, contemplatives in love with God.

(Pope John Paul II)

I stand by the title I have chosen for this chapter, though I realise that it could be misleading. It might seem to suggest, for example, that since becoming a prison chaplain I have acquired a vast store of brand-new knowledge. In fact, there have not been many new lessons. For the most part it has been old, but vitally important, lessons learned afresh, hammered home with new intensity in special circumstances. Indeed – and here again the title could mislead – I would not wish to claim that the lessons have been mastered even now. I am a slow learner, I need to be taught the same things over and over again. Fortunately, I do not seem to be alone in this respect. And so I hope that not only for me but also for many of my readers – especially those who recognise that through baptism they share in the missionary outreach of the Church – this chapter may provide the opportunity for some useful re-thinking.

'Love tenderly'

Let me go back to the beginning – my first Sunday in prison more than twenty years ago. The service which I led on that occasion is one that I shall never forget. Not because it was the first prison celebration in which I had ever participated, but for an altogether different reason: because of an unexpected event which took place.

When I went into the vestry that morning to get ready for Mass, I laid on the vesting bench two books, one was a Breviary (a book of daily prayers) and the other a well-known spiritual reading book. At the end of Mass, I was vaguely aware that the small pile of books had been reduced still further, but it was not until I got home at lunch time that I realised that the spiritual reading book was missing. I returned to the prison to look for it, but without success.

As a last resort, I decided to have a chat with my red-band sacristan, to enquire if by any chance he had seen the missing book, which I described to him in some detail. He began to grin, and I suspected that I had already found the culprit, but he assured me: 'Honestly, I haven't touched it. But I know what's happened. Someone's nicked it, and they're not half in for a let-down, aren't they?' Then it was my turn to laugh, for it suddenly dawned upon me that the book, written by the contemplative monk Father Eugene Boylan, had a title which was open to more than one interpretation. It was called *This Tremendous Lover*. The borrower of the book – he had not really stolen it, for it turned up mysteriously in my office a few days later – had obviously thought that he was on to something sensational, a sizzling, hot-blooded romance. Though heaven knows what he must have thought of the new chaplain who indulged in such reading – and in the vestry, too!

I say that I laughed. The incident certainly had its amusing side, but it seemed to me that it had its sad side as well. 'Poor lad', I found myself thinking, as I reflected on the phantom borrower. 'He's probably never thought of God as a tremendous lover; just supposing he had ... ' It was at that moment that my reflections were cut short, as the Lord began teaching me my very first lesson 'inside'. It came in the form of a question, which slowly took shape in my mind: 'Never mind him, what about you? Are you really convinced that God is a tremendous lover?' It is so easy to pay lip-service to such notions. How hard genuinely to believe them!

And yet, on reflection, there does not seem much point in trying to serve the Lord in the prison ministry, or in any other, unless we are convinced that he loves us – deeply and dearly, tenderly and tremendously. No one has ever expressed the idea more impressively than did St Paul. He was in a prison cell when he wrote about the length and the breadth, the height and the depth of God's love for us (Eph 3:18). His words have always made me think of one of those tea-chests with a label marked 'FRAGILE' on the outside, and on the inside endless packing material to safeguard the precious goods. St Paul is assuring us that we are precious in God's sight; that is why he envelops us on every side with his love – above, below, to right, to left. We are precious, but enormously fragile, too: how could we ever offer ourselves for any apostolate if it depended upon our own goodness? The embarrassing yet comforting truth is that God does not chose us for a ministry because we deserve to be chosen, but simply because he loves us and wants to use us in this particular way – despite the weakness and inadequacy and sinfulness.

However, there is what might be called a flip-side to all this. It is hard enough for me to believe that God loves me in the undeserved, no-holds-barred kind of way just described. But to accept that he loves other people in exactly in the same way? And not just some people, the obviously nice and decent and good people, but all the people, every man, woman and child I shall ever meet. Most prisoners, as I indicated in the first chapter of this book, are society's 'damaged goods'. On the whole, damaged goods are not instantly attractive; they tend to be left on the shelves and sold cheap. But when the damaged goods are people, we are invited to examine them more closely and to discover that their essential dignity remains undimmed. Indeed the Christian is challenged to visualise on such damaged goods a label which reads: 'Tenderly loved by God'; even more – and this can cost him dearly – he is called to love them himself and to love them as God loves them: 'By this will all men know that you are my disciples, if you have love for one another' (Jn 13:35). To love them, especially when they have known very little love in their lives, is a powerful way, perhaps the only way, of leading them to the discovery that God loves them, too.

'Act justly'

Too much talk about loving people runs the danger of substituting vague words for practical action. One of the lessons I have learned – or re-learned – in prison is the value of thinking of what we do for others in terms of justice: we *owe* it to them to treat them as brothers and sisters in Christ. St Louise de Marillac, a close associate of St Vincent de Paul in his heroic work for the outcasts of society, used to plead: 'Let us give the best we have to the poor since it is theirs *by right*'. And the 'best we have' refers not only to material goods, but to the whole attitude we adopt to the poor in our midst.

In a previous chapter I presented some of the characteristics of my Average Prisoner. Perhaps the time has come to attempt a companion picture of some of the qualities one would hope to find in the 'just' prison chaplain. Indeed, in view of what was said earlier about the universal nature of the prison ministry (see page 123), it is clear that this companion picture reflects all those – whether they be priests or lay people, women or men – who minister to the imprisoned. Probably the picture has already begun to emerge from the earlier part of this book, but it may be useful to highlight a few of its features. Here they are;

• The 'just' chaplain is sincerely compassionate. There is no place in prison for softness or sentimentality, but he knows that he owes his flock a genuine and deep-down concern, and that true gentleness is a sign of strength, not of weakness. He knows too that being on the receiving end of another's pastoral ministry can be as difficult as being on the receiving end of another's charity: it can hurt and give rise to feelings of inferiority. It is particularly important, therefore, for a chaplain to avoid a patronising attitude in his dealings with others. They are his brothers and sisters, his equals. Similarly, as has often been acknowledged in chaplaincy circles, he owes it to them to be a true professional, in the sense of being competent and confident in his work: they deserve better than a bumbling amateur, however well intentioned he may be. But equally he owes it to them not to become the kind of phoney professional who is more interested in courses and techniques and psychological theories than in people. 'Oh, Jesus', wrote a long-term prisoner in a letter to *The Times*, 'how one misses a bit of loving kindness instead of this god-awful welfare.'

• He has great resources of patience and perseverance. For several years four nuns and I ran a number of small discussion groups for young prisoners. At the end of each term we came together for 'our family Mass', a fairly informal celebration which the youngsters themselves helped to prepare, by choosing readings, writing their own Bidding Prayers, and so on. The Mass was followed by refreshments, rather grandly styled an 'Agape', consisting of tea and biscuits, sweets and cigarettes. It had always proved a great success; which was why we were all shattered – and I roused to anger – when, at the end of one term, a group which had already given us many headaches in the preceding weeks behaved extremely badly at the 'family Mass', turning it into a big laugh from beginning to end. I was all for ensuring that they would never get the chance to do that again: there would be no more end-of-term Masses or Agapes. Though I simmered down later, almost every time the Sisters and I met we got round to discussing what we should do at the end of the next term. One of the Sisters, a quite outstanding person, never said very much, yet in an extraordinary way won us all round to the idea that we should 'go ahead as though nothing untoward had happened'. We did so. The celebration could hardly have gone better; and at the Agape one of the lads, on his own initiative, stood up and made a little speech of apology on behalf of the group; and everyone enjoyed themselves; and I was given a valuable lesson in patience.

On the same theme but on a lighter note, the longest serving chaplain currently in post often recalls how he one day visited a man on the punishment block, who turned his face to the wall and snapped: 'Get lost'. (I have to confess that they were not the precise words, but they were two other monosyllabic words with much the same meaning!) The following day the chaplain visited again, to be met with a similar response, except that this time the 'Get lost' (or its equivalent) was suitably strengthened with other expletives. The next day the chaplain was off duty, but the day after he faithfully returned to the punishment block. As he opened the door, he found to his surprise that the prisoner was waiting to speak to him; he was even more surprised, when he heard what the prisoner had to say: 'Chaplain, where the hell were you yesterday?'!

• He gladly recalls that kindness is one of the special gifts which denotes the presence of the Holy Spirit (Gal 5:22), and he prays that he may have it in full measure. I have already had occasion to mention the importance of small things in prison life, like the way you unlock a door.

Many chaplains can testify that kindnesses, even quite small kindnesses, are remembered gratefully by prisoners long after they have been forgotten by the person responsible for them. Vincent de Paul, a saint with first-hand knowledge of prisoners, used to tell his friends: 'Kindness is the key to all hearts'. And the passage of the years, as every chaplain knows, has done nothing to diminish the validity of those words.

● He sees the need to be an optimist, he owes it to his parishioners to be ready to see the good in them, even when it is little more than a spark. In *The Gulag Archipelago*, the story of prisoners and slave labour camps in Russia, Alexander Solzhenitsyn recounts how a woman prisoner was being taken for interrogation by an impassive, silent, apparently inhuman guard, when bombs suddenly began to drop in the vicinity of the prison. At that moment, all the brutality left the guard, she threw her arms round the prisoner and embraced her, she was desperate for human companionship and support. Then the bombing stopped, and at once she reverted to type, as she roared: 'Hands behind your back! Move along!' Solzhenitsyn remarks, rather icily: 'Well, of course, there was no great merit in that – to become a human being at the moment of death'. But, I wonder? Is not this incident intensely moving because it is so unexpected? And ought we not always to be ready to rejoice when we catch sight of a glimpse of goodness, the more so when it is in unlikely people or in unlikely circumstances?

Solzhenitsyn offers an extreme example, but I, like many a prison chaplain, can provide many humbler ones, like the day when my red-band (not the 'Tremendous Lover' one) came into my office. He was a rather shy, inarticulate fellow. Digging deep into his pocket he produced a chocolate biscuit and placed it on the desk. 'That's for you!' he blurted out. 'But really, Peter', I said, 'I'm fine, I don't need it.' 'Still, I want you to have it', he insisted. 'I get two every day and I know you have none to eat with your coffee in the afternoon; do take it.' I did take the chocolate biscuit and it meant more to me than Peter could ever realise. If, as the old hymn has it, 'where love is, there is God', then surely God was present and at work in my office that day.

Every flash of goodness in others is by way of gentle reminder that God cares for them. I said earlier that we need to be optimists; but it is an optimism that is the fruit of deep faith, which assures us that the transforming power of the Holy Spirit 'can do infinitely more than we can ask or imagine' (Eph 3:20), however worthless and futile our own efforts seem to be.

● And if he has a sense of humour, it helps. Not that he is necessarily a born comedian, but rather that he has the knack of seeing the lighter side of things. A sense of humour can often ease tense situations, cement relationships, be a way of revealing to others our real humanity, and it can also be a great protection against taking ourselves too seriously. I like the story of good Pope John who in the early period of his pontificate was pacing up and down his bedroom, unable to sleep because of the burden of cares pressing down upon him, when suddenly a voice was heard. It was the voice of the Lord. 'All right, Holy Father', it said, 'you go to bed now and I'll stay up for the rest of the night.' The story may be apocryphal, but its message is too good to be ignored, especially by those who can feel themselves overwhelmed by the difficulties and disappointments of the prison apostolate.

'Walk humbly'

In prison I have been taught time and again the lesson of love (God does love me tremendously, and all my friends 'inside' in the same boundless way). Similarly I have learned the lesson of justice (I owe it to them to be compassionate and sincere and patient and optimistic, with an eye to small kindnesses, and – if I am blessed that way – with a sense of humour, to help them and me on our way). But there is another lesson that has been inescapable in prison, the lesson of humility. It is not only the realisation of one's own limitations that pricks one's pride. It is also the fearful contrast that exists between the advantages one has onself experienced in life and the disadvantages that so many prisoners have had to endure.

I think, for example, of Andrew. When, during an interview, I mentioned his mother, he reacted with a vehemence that was totally unexpected. Most prisoners hold Mum in high regard, whatever they may think of other people; but Andrew stated flatly: 'Don't speak to me about that woman. I hate her'. And then went on to talk about her himself. The story that was unfolded told of how Andrew's mother had been a prostitute. How on one occasion, when he discovered her with one of her lovers and began to cry because he thought she was being attacked, his mother 'got up and knocked the living daylights out of me'. How on another occasion she left him, then only five, and his little sister alone in the house for three days, with nothing on but a vest, 'which came down to here', he added as he pointed to his midriff.

I think of Andrew and ask myself: if I had had his early experiences in life, would I now be ministering or being ministered to in prison?

Or I think of Harry, a drug addict since fifteen, who almost lost a leg because of an infection picked up from the use of non-sterile needles. He has fought and keeps on fighting his addiction. Once I went to see him in hospital where he was thought to be dying. He had the New Testament perched on his bedside table. It was the only book he seemed to read and he said it brought him much comfort. 'Do you know' he said, 'if I were to die tonight, even though it's through dabbling in drugs, and so, I suppose, through my own fault, I still wouldn't despair; I'd die trusting in Jesus.'

I think of Harry and ask myself: If I had fought so tenaciously with such little success for so long, would my trust in the Lord be as sturdy as his?

Or I think of Danny. When he first came to prison we got round to talking about prayer. I asked him if he prayed. 'Oh yes', he replied, 'I do pray. I pray to God, and I pray to our Lady – and sometimes I pray to St Jude.' The final words came as a surprise. 'Do you know anything about St Jude?' I enquired. Somewhat diffidently, he reported that he understood Jude was an apostle and also some kind of relative of our Lord and that he had written part of the New Testament, 'and', he added more confidently, 'he's the patron saint of hopeless cases'. Perhaps I should not have done it, but I could not resist putting the question: 'And what about you, Danny? do you think you're a hopeless case?' With the utmost simplicity – with a marvellous kind of innocence – he replied: 'Yes, I do'.

I think of Danny and of how his candour seemed to pierce my heart and I find myself saying: prison seems to be one of the best places in the world for realising that we are all hopeless cases, we are all sinners. The Lord himself has pointed out, in the final Judgement, when at last absolute justice will be achieved, there may be some strange reversals of fortunes – especially for religious leaders.

In the light of all that I have said in this chapter it should come as no surprise when I add that work in prison has taught me again the need I have of Christ's help. 'I can do all things in him who strengthens me' (Phil 4:13; RSV). But if I want that strength I must meet him in prayer. Richard Wurmbrand, the heroic Rumanian pastor, who himself spent fourteen years in Communist prisons, tells a tremendous story about a fellow pastor. He had been imprisoned for his faith and found himself sharing a cell with a former Communist goaler and torturer, who had himself fallen foul of the system. The two men became close friends, largely through the great charity of the pastor, who not only spoke of Christ but also gave a share of his meagre diet to his companion day by day. Eventually the Communist begged him not to go on talking about Christ. 'Just tell me', he said, 'in a nutshell what is this Jesus Christ really like?' There was a moment of silence before the pastor quietly replied: 'He is like me'. And then came the wonderful rejoinder: 'In that case I can love him with all my heart and trust him'.

There are very few who would have the boldness of that pastor, yet many of us know only too well that our way of living ought to be such that other men and women are brought to a better understanding of Christ the Lord; and in our hearts of hearts we also know that without prayer our lives will be shallow and sterile. Unless we learn the lesson of prayer, we shall not learn the lesson of love, or the lesson of treating others justly and fairly, or the lesson of humility. Unless we are prepared to walk with our God in prayer then we might as well give up attempting the impossible.

At the beginning of this chapter, I made it clear that I am a slow learner, and, as I reach the end, I am even more convinced that I have a lot more learning to do. But may I also insist, as I did at the start, that the lessons I have been presenting are in no sense new. In fact they are lessons that were being taught some seven or eight centuries before Our Lord was born by the prophet Micah who has left us these remarkable words:

> This is what the Lord asks of you:
> only this, to act *justly*,
> to *love* tenderly
> and to walk *humbly* with your God. (Mic 6:8)

A superb one-sentence job description for anyone called to the pastoral ministry and not least for one called to the ministry of prison chaplain.

APPENDIXES

APPENDIX A

Structure of the UK Prison Service Chaplaincy at Headquarters

Today there is a united Prison Service Chaplaincy of more than 400 full-time and part-time chaplains from the Anglican, Methodist and Roman Catholic churches. The first step towards the present organisation was taken in 1896 when the chaplain of Holloway Prison was appointed Visiting Chaplain to Her Majesty's Prisons, with the task of assisting the Commissioners in the selection of suitable candidates as chaplains, visiting prisons to see that religious services were 'conducted with zeal and that the duties of Chaplains...and school masters are properly carried out...to see that prisoners' libraries are suitably kept up' and 'occasionally to preach in the prison chapels' (*Prison Commissioners Report 1896*). In 1902 the holder of the post was renamed Chaplain Inspector and in 1950 the last of the Chaplain Inspectors took up a full-time appointment at Headquarters. Twelve years later the title of Chaplain Inspector was replaced by that of Chaplain General of Prisons.

The *Chaplain General* stands at the head of the Prison Service Chaplaincy; he provides leadership and oversight in co-operation with the Principal Roman Catholic and the Superintendent Methodist Chaplains. Since 1963 he has had the assistance of another senior chaplain who is now designated the *Deputy Chaplain General*.

The third chaplain working and stationed at headquarters is the *Principal Roman Catholic Chaplain*: his post (though under a slightly different title) was created in 1957 but it was not until 1973 that the postholder began a full-time headquarters partnership with the Chaplain General and Deputy Chaplain General. He is the senior representative of his Church in the Prison Department, with special responsibility for Roman Catholic Chaplains and all matters of specifically Roman Catholic concern. Five other chaplains, though not stationed at headquarters, form part of the chaplaincy headquarters group. They are the three *Assistant Chaplains General* who have operational responsibility so far as all Church of England chaplains are concerned, and two *Senior Roman Catholic Chaplains*, who regularly visit all Roman Catholic chaplains in the field and, like their Anglican counterparts, provide support and guidance.

Traditionally the Methodist Church has nominated a Methodist Chaplain for each prison to care for all Free Church prisoners, but since they form such a small proportion of the prison population there are no full-time Methodist chaplains. However, the Methodist Church appoints a *Superintendent Methodist Chaplain* on a full-time basis; he is a member of the Home Mission

Division which represents chaplaincy concerns to the Methodist Conference. He carries special responsibility for Methodist Chaplains and Methodist issues within the Prison Service, visits prisons throughout the country and has close links with the other members of the Chaplaincy headquarters team.

APPENDIX B

BRITISH PENAL INSTITUTIONS
as at January 1987

England & Wales

All are prisons unless otherwise indicated. Abbreviations are as follows:

DC	Detention Centre	F	Female
RC	Remand Centre	M	Male
YCC	Youth Custody Centre		
YO	Young Offenders		

1	Acklington, Northumberland		63	Blundeston, Suffolk
2	Castington, Northumberland	YCC	64	Wayland, Norfolk
3	Medomsley, Co. Durham	DC	65	Highpoint, Suffolk
4	Frankland, Durham		66	Hollesley Bay Colony, Suffolk
5	Low Newton, Co. Durham	RC; F & M under 21	67	Chelmsford
			68	Bullwood Hall, Essex
6	Durham	with F secure wing	69	Campsfield House, Oxfordshire
			70	Oxford
7	Deerbolt, Co. Durham	YCC	71	Grendon, Buckinghamshire
8	Kirklevington Grange, Cleveland	DC	72	Spring Hill, Buckinghamshire
9	Northallerton, N. Yorks	YCC	73	Aylesbury, Buckinghamshire
10	Haverigg Camp, Cumbria		74	Huntercombe, Oxfordshire
11	Lancaster		75	Finnamore Wood, Buckinghamshire
12	Kirkham, Preston		76	Reading
13	Preston		77	Ashford, Middlesex
14	Wymott, Preston		78	Feltham, Middlesex
15	Buckley Hall, Rochdale	DC	79	Wormwood Scrubs, London W12
16	Liverpool	with YO wing	80	Holloway, London N7
17	Hindley, Wigan	YCC	81	Pentonville, London N7
18	Risley, Warrington	RC; F & M under 21	82	Latchmere House, Surrey
19	Thorn Cross, Warrington	YCC	83	Wandsworth, London SW18
20	Manchester	with YO wing	84	Brixton, London SW2
21	Styal, Cheshire	F & YCC	85	Coldingley, Surrey
22	Rudgate, Wetherby		86	Send, Surrey
23	Askham Grange, York	F	87	Rochester, Kent
24	Wetherby	YCC	88	Cookham Wood, Kent
25	Thorp Arch, Wetherby		89	Maidstone, Kent
26	Leeds		90	East Sutton Park, Kent
27	Wakefield		91	Standford Hill, Kent
28	New Hall, Wakefield	DC	92	Canterbury
29	Everthorpe, N. Humberside	YCC	93	Dover
30	Hull	with RC for under 21s	94	Aldington, Kent
31	Hatfield, Doncaster	YCC	95	Blantyre House, Kent
32	Lindholme, Doncaster		96	Northeye, East Sussex
33	Gringley, Doncaster	DC	97	Lewes, East Sussex
34	Ranby, Nottinghamshire		98	Ford, West Sussex
35	Lincoln		99	Winchester
36	Morton Hall, Lincoln			
37	Shrewsbury		100	Haslar, Hants
38	Stoke Heath, Shropshire	YCC	101	Kingston, Portsmouth
39	Werrington, Stoke-on-Trent	YCC	102	Parkhurst, Isle of Wight
40	Drake Hall, Staffordshire	F	103	Albany, Isle of Wight
41	Stafford		104	Camp Hill, Isle of Wight
42	Featherstone, Wolverhampton		105	Swansea
43	Sudbury, Derby			
44	Foston Hall, Derby	DC	106	Cardiff
45	Swinfen Hall, Staffordshire	YCC		
46	Birmingham		107	Usk, Gwent
47	Hewell Grange, Worcestershire	YCC	108	Gloucester
48	Brockhill, Worcestershire	RC	109	Eastwood Park, Gloucestershire
49	Long Lartin, Worcestershire		110	Leyhill, Gloucestershire
50	Nottingham		111	Pucklechurch, Bristol
51	Lowdham Grange, Nottingham	YCC		
52	Whatton, Nottingham	DC	112	Bristol
53	Ashwell, Leicestershire		113	Erlestoke House, Wiltshire
54	Stocken, Leicestershire		114	Shepton Mallet, Somerset
55	Leicester		115	Guys Marsh, Dorset
56	Glen Parva, Leicestershire	YCC & RC	116	Dorchester
57	Gartree, Leicestershire			
58	Onley, Warwickshire	YCC	117	The Verne, Dorset
59	Wellingborough, Northants	YCC	118	Portland, Dorset
60	Bedford		119	Exeter
61	North Sea Camp, Lincolnshire	DC		
62	Norwich	with RC for under 21s	120	Channings Wood, Devon
			121	Dartmoor

Right column abbreviations:

66	Hollesley Bay Colony, Suffolk	YCC & DC
67	Chelmsford	YO & RC
68	Bullwood Hall, Essex	F & YCC
69	Campsfield House, Oxfordshire	YCC
71	Grendon, Buckinghamshire	with YCC
73	Aylesbury, Buckinghamshire	YCC
74	Huntercombe, Oxfordshire	YCC
75	Finnamore Wood, Buckinghamshire	YCC
77	Ashford, Middlesex	RC
78	Feltham, Middlesex	YCC
80	Holloway, London N7	F
82	Latchmere House, Surrey	RC, M under 21
87	Rochester, Kent	YCC
88	Cookham Wood, Kent	F & YCC
90	East Sutton Park, Kent	F & YCC
93	Dover	YCC
95	Blantyre House, Kent	DC
99	Winchester	with RC for under 21s
100	Haslar, Hants	DC
105	Swansea	with RC for under 21s
106	Cardiff	with RC for under 21s
107	Usk, Gwent	YCC & DC
109	Eastwood Park, Gloucestershire	DC
111	Pucklechurch, Bristol	RC; F & M under 21
113	Erlestoke House, Wiltshire	YCC & DC
115	Guys Marsh, Dorset	YCC
116	Dorchester	with RC for under 21s
118	Portland, Dorset	YCC
119	Exeter	with YCC & RC for under 21s

Scotland and Northern Ireland

1	Inverness		20	Magilligan, Co. Londonderry	
2	Peterhead, Aberdeenshire		21	Belfast (Crumlin Road)	
3	Aberdeen		22	Belfast (Hydebank Wood)	YO
4	Noranside, Angus	YO	23	Maze, Co. Antrim	
5	Castle Huntly, Dundee	YO	24	Maghaberry, Co. Antrim	M & F
6	Perth				
7	Friarton, Perth				
8	Glenochil, Clackmannanshire	YO & DC			
9	Cornton Vale, Stirlingshire	F			
10	Greenock, Renfrewshire				
11	Low Moss, Glasgow				
12	Barlinnie, Glasgow				
13	Dungavel, Lanarkshire				
14	Longriggend, Lanarkshire	RC			
15	Polmont, Stirlingshire	YO			
16	Shotts, Lanarkshire				
17	Edinburgh				
18	Dumfries				
19	Penninghame, Wigtownshire				

NOTES

NOTES

2. ROOTED IN THE GOSPELS

1. *Silent Pilgrimage to God* (Darton, Longman and Todd, 1974), p. 42.
2. *Spiritual Autobiography of Charles de Foucauld*, edited by Jean François Six (Dimension Books, New York), p. 147.
3. A phrase coined by Martin Kähler in 1892.
4. Rowan Williams, *Resurrection* (Darton, Longman and Todd, 1982), p. 19.
5. Karl Rahner, *Mission and Grace*, vol. III (Sheed and Ward, 1966), pp. 77, 78.
6. W. D. Davies, *Invitation to the New Testament* (1967), p. 227.
7. Roy Kilner, *New Life* (prison chaplaincy review) (1985), p. 27.
8. Since about 1300 the Catholic Church has celebrated, every quarter of a century, a 'Holy Year', drawing its inspiration from the old Jewish custom of the 'year of Jubilee' when slaves and captives were to be set free (cf. Leviticus chapter 25).
9. P. Hebblethwaite, *The Year of the Three Popes* (Collins, 1979), p. 119.

3. PENAL HISTORY AND THE PRISON CHAPLAIN

1. S. McConville, *A History of English Prison Administration*, vol. I (Routledge & Kegan Paul, 1981), pp. 22, 23.
2. *Ibid.*, p. 9.
3. J. H. Plumb, *The First Four Georges* (Fontana/Collins, 1976), p. 16.
4. Major A. Griffiths, *Memorials of Millbank*, vol. I (1875), p. 33.
5. Dr H. Tomlinson, 'The 1878 Inheritance', *Prison Service Journal*, no. 31, (1987), p. 10.
6. Janet Whitney, *Elizabeth Fry* (Harrap, 1937), pp. 184, 185.
7. *Prison Rules* (1843) and R. S. E. Hinde, *The British Penal System 1773–1950* (Duckworth, 1951), *passim*.
8. The Reverend Dr C. Copley, 'The Role and Function of the Prison Chaplain' (unpublished thesis), p. 44.
9. D. L. Howard, *The English Prisons* (Methuen, 1960), p. 105.
10. K. Chesney, *The Victorian Underworld* (Pelican, 1972), p. 22.
11. K. Chesney, *ibid*, p. 24, quoting Mayhew and Binney, *The Criminal Prisons of London*, p. 304.
12. Rev. J. M. Tweedy, *Popish Elvet* (Quisgan Printers Ltd, Tyneside, undated), p. 46.

13. Quoted by Director General in address at the AGM of the Institute for the Study and Treatment of Delinquency (1 December 1976).
14. From S. Hobhouse and A. Fenner Brockway, *English Prisons Today* (Longmans, 1922); quoted by L. Fox, *The English Prison and Borstal Systems* (London, 1952), p. 62.
15. Statement of Sir Alexander Maxwell, Permanent Under-Secretary at the time of Paterson's death.
16. From Preface of *Paterson on Prisons*, edited by S. K. Ruck (1961).
17. K. Neale, 'Her Majesty's Commissioners 1878–1978' (for private circulation), p. 24.
18. Cf. *The Sentence of the Court* (HMSO, 1964).
19. The Council for Social Welfare, *The Prison System* (Dublin, 1983), p. 5.
20. K. Neale, *op. cit.*, p. 54.
21. *Macbeth* III, v, 32.
22. L. Fox, *The English Prison and Borstal Systems* (London, 1952), p. 201.
23. Assistant governors, successors to the borstal 'housemasters', made their appearance in 1949; probation officers were not introduced until 1966, though there had been welfare officers since 1955, and social workers before that; psychologists appeared on the prison scene in 1946; and, after a pioneer scheme in the Durham area in 1944, LEAs began to provide education officers (or 'tutor organisers' as they were called at first) for all penal establishments.
24. *Memorials of Millbank*, vol. I, p. 196; quoted by N. McLachlan in *Progress in Penal Reform*, edited by L. Blom-Cooper (Clarendon Press, 1974).
25. On 12 July 1985 the prison population stood at 48,037, the highest in British history up to that date.
26. Sir Rupert Cross in the Hamlyn Lectures of 1971.

4. PRISON PARISH

1. Preface to *English Prisons under Local Government* by Sidney and Beatrice Webb (Longmans, 1932).
2. The two pioneering works in this area are: Donald Clemmer, *The Prison Community* (New York, 1940) and Gresham Sykes, *Society of Captives* (Princeton, 1958). Sykes, in chapter IV, speaks of a five-fold deprivation which prisoners face: that of (i) liberty (and therefore social acceptance); (ii) goods and services (i.e. material possessions); (iii) heterosexual relationships; (iv) personal autonomy and (v) personal security.
3. Erving Goffman, *Asylums* (Doubleday, 1961).
4. Tom Tickell, *Observer Magazine* (20 February 1977).
5. Quoted in S. McConville, *A History of English Prison Administration*, vol. I (Routledge and Kegan Paul, 1981), p. 118.
6. These remarks were made in a BBC television interview a few years ago, though I have been unable to discover the precise date or the name of the programme.
7. J. E. Hall Williams, *Changing Prisons* (Peter Owen, 1975), p. 163.
8. As a minimum, prisoners under twenty-one have fortnightly visits, convicted prisoners one visit every twenty-eight days, but some prisons allow more than the strict minimum.
   Prisoners may also send and receive one letter per week, though further letters may be allowed if the prisoners pay for them themselves.
9. House of Commons Expenditure Committee (1978).

10. This information I owe to an article by Père A. Clavier, chaplain of La Santé, in *Lettre aux Aumôniers de Prison* (May/June 1985).
11. Mr W. Driscoll, governor of Walton prison, Liverpool in the BBC2 programme *A Life with Crime* (1 April 1979); quoted in H. Jones, *Society against Crime* (Penguin Books, 1981), p. 170.
12. Martin Wright, *Making Good* (Burnett Books, 1982), p. 44.
13. *Annual Report of H.M. Inspector of Prisons* (HMSO, 1981).
14. Gresham Sykes, *op. cit.*, p. 107.
15. Jimmy Boyle, *A Sense of Freedom* (Pan Books, 1977), p. 107.
16. Audrey Peckham, *A Woman in Custody* (Fontana, 1985), p. 70.
17. Rule 1.
18. S. McConville, *op. cit.*, pp. 187ff.
19. John Heywood, quoted in *People in Prison* (Cmnd 4214; HMSO, 1969), §15.
20. *The Chaplaincy Contribution to Penal Thought and Practice* (report of seminar; Home Office Prison Department, 1980), pp. 6ff.

5. PRISON PARISHIONERS

1. Quoted by Little Brother Peter in *Jesus Caritas*, no. 58, p. 33.
2. *The Chaplaincy Contribution to Penal Thought and Practice* (Home Office Prison Department, 1980), p. 6.
3. *The Merchant of Venice* III, i, 63.
4. Prisoner's comment in a paper written by Sister Joan Barry.
5. *Report on the Work of the Prison Department 1979* (Cmnd 7965; HMSO, 1980), §95, though the more recent *Annual Report 1984/5* (Cmnd 9699; HMSO, 1985), §227, reports only 9 per cent in the ten or under reading age.
6. *The Grendon Experiment*, BBC2 (November 1984).
7. Dr. R. Hewland, *New Zealand Prison Chaplains' Association Magazine* (November 1985), p. 16.
8. Joanna Kelley, *Who Casts the First Stone?* (Epworth Press, 1978), p. 10.
9. In an unpublished essay by the Reverend R. Payne, currently Chaplaincy Training Officer.
10. Cf. Susan Edwards, *Woman on Trial* (Manchester University Press, 1985).
11. *The Social Consequences to the Wives and Family of a Man in Prison*, a joint report by three organisations, Helping Hand, Apex and the Circle Trust (December 1968).
12. *Report of Her Majesty's Inspector of Prisons 1984* (HMSO, 1985), §2.26.
13. *Report on the Work of the Prison Department 1984/5* (Cmnd 9699, HMSO, 1985), §73.
14. S. Milgram, *Obedience to Authority* (Tavistock, 1974); C. Banks, C. Haney and P. Zimbardo, 'Interpersonal Dynamics in a Simulated Prison', *International Journal of Criminology and Penology*, vol. I (1973).
15. J. Boyle, *A Sense of Freedom* (Pan Books, 1977), p. 191.
16. *Report of Her Majesty's Inspector of Prisons 1984*, *op. cit.*
17. Father Tim Curtis, SJ.
18. J. Vanier, 'To my Brothers and Sisters in Prison', *Les Chemins de l'Arche – La Ferme.*

6. PRISON PASTOR

1. *A Charter for Prison Chaplains* (Strasbourg, 1983).

2. Paul Tillich, *The Shaking of the Foundations* (Penguin Books, 1962), p. 163.
3. *Constitution on the Sacred Liturgy*, art. 10: *The Documents of Vatican II*, ed. W. M. Abbott, SJ (Geoffrey Chapman, 1966).
4. Karl Rahner, *Mission and Grace*, vol. III (Sheed & Ward Stagbooks, 1966), pp. 89f.
5. Gregory Baum, *Chaplains' Newsletter* (November 1973), p. 9.
6. Reverend A. Hughes in *The Catholic Herald* (February 1986).
7. 'Report to the Bishops of Ireland on the Prison Ministry' (typescript; 1980).
8. Archbishop Joseph L. Bernardin, *Called to Serve, Called to Lead* (St Anthony Messenger Press, 1981), p. 20.
9. P. Berger, *A Rumour of Angels* (Doubleday Anchor Books, 1970).
10. P. Lehmann, *Ethics in a Christian Context* (SCM Press, 1963).
11. 'Zeno', *Life* (Macmillan, 1968).
12. J. V. Taylor, *The Go-Between God* (SCM Press, 1972), p. 69.

7. *FOCUSING ON CRIME*

1. *Pastoral Constitution on the Church in the Modern World*, art. 62: *The Documents of Vatican II*, ed. W. M. Abbott, SJ (Geoffrey Chapman, 1966).
2. T. Morris, 'Crime and Criminology', *British Journal of Sociology* (December 1965), p. 358.
3. C. de Beccaria, *An Essay on Crimes and Punishment* (1801), esp. ch. I.
4. W. S. Gilbert, *The Mikado*, Act II.
5. Dr C. Goring, *The English Convict* (HMSO, 1913).
6. H. Eysenck, *Crime and Personality* (Paladin, 1970).
7. I. Taylor, P. Walton and J. Young, *The New Criminology* (Routledge and Kegan Paul, 1973), pp. 47–66.
8. R. K. Merton, 'Social Structures and Anomie', *American Sociological Review*, III (1938), 672–682.
9. L. Taylor, *Deviance and Society* (Michael Joseph, 1971), pp. 124–125.
10. A. Cohen, *Delinquent Boys: The Culture of the Gang* (Free Press, Chicago, 1955).
11. R. Cloward and L. Ohlin, *Delinquency and Opportunity* (Free Press, 1960).
12. W. B. Miller, 'Lower Class Culture as a Generating Milieu of Gang Delinquency', *Journal of Social Issues*, XV (1958).
13. D. Matza, *Delinquency and Drift* (John Wiley, 1964).
14. D. M. Downes, *The Delinquent Solution* (Routledge and Kegan Paul, 1966).
15. H. Becker, *Outsiders* (Free Press, 1963).
16. I. Taylor, P. Walton and J. Young, *op. cit.*
17. Jenifer Hart, 'Why Do Women Commit Less Crime?', *New Society* (30 August 1985), pp. 298ff.
18. J. Mortimer in *The Sunday Times* (27 March 1983).
19. A. Keith Bottomley, *Criminology in Focus* (Martin Robertson, 1979), p. 62.
20. T. Morris, *Deviance and Control* (Hutchinson, 1976), p. 95.
21. H. S. Kushner, *When Bad Things Happen to Good People* (Pan Books, 1982), p. 91.
22. L. Williams in Appendix to A. Von Hirsch, *Doing Justice: The Choice of Punishments* (Hill and Wang, New York, 1976), p. 178.
23. N. Ward, *Five for Sorrow, Ten for Joy* (Epworth Press, 1971), p. 20.
24. D. Rhymes, *Prayer in the Secular City* (Lutterworth Press, 1967), p. 67.
25. J. Mahoney, SJ, *Seeking the Spirit* (Sheed and Ward Dimension Books, 1981), p. 37.

26. E. Sutherland, *Principles of Criminology* (Chicago, 1924); revised as E. Sutherland and D. Cressey, *Criminology* (New York, 1979).
27. J. Mahoney, *op. cit.*, p. 38.

8. *PUNISH AND BE DAMNED?*

1. Peter Evans, *Prison Crisis* (Allen and Unwin, 1980), p. 159.
2. Ernest Van den Haag, *Punishing Criminals* (Basic Books, New York, 1975).
3. William Temple, *The Ethics of Punishment* (1930).
4. A. Bottoms, *The Coming Penal Crisis* (Scottish Academic Press, 1980), p. 1.
5. Cf. especially the research of R. Martinson and his associates for the USA (1974) and S. Brody for the UK (1976).
6. David Fogel, Commissioner of Corrections in Minnesota (1971–73), seems to have coined this expression.
7. An expression of J. Rawls, *A Theory of Justice* (Oxford University Press, 1972), and used by D. Fogel.
8. Quintin Hogg in the Parliamentary Debate on the 1969 Criminal Justice Act, quoted by Philip Bean, *Punishment* (Martin Robertson, 1981).
9. Norval Morris, *The Future of Imprisonment* (University of Chicago, 1974).
10. Frank Pakenham, Lord Longford, *The Idea of Punishment* (Geoffrey Chapman, 1961), p. 27.
11. C. S. Lewis, 'The Humanitarian Theory of Punishment', *Res Judicatae*, 6 (1953), p. 225.
12. Elizabeth Moberly, *Suffering, Innocent and Guilty* (SPCK, 1978), p. 94.
13. Gordon Dunstan, *New Life* (prison chaplaincy review), (1980), p. 51.
14. *The Chaplaincy Contribution to Penal Thought and Practice* (report of seminar; Home Office Prison Department, 1980), p. 6.
15. Alexander Solzhenitsyn, *The Gulag Archipelago* (Fontana, 1974), p. 168.
16. *Punishment and Imprisonment* (Dominican Publications, Dublin, 1985), p. 32.
17. Leon Radzinowicz and Joan King, *The Growth of Crime* (Penguin Books, 1979), p. 62.
18. Reported by prison governor Michael Jenkins, *Crime and the Responsible Community* (Hodder and Stoughton, 1980), p. 135.
19. *New Society* (1985), p. 447.
20. *Black People in the Criminal Justice System* (NACRO information document).
21. *Prisons and Prisoners in England Today* (Church Information Office, 1978), §58.
22. Bishop Dozier, *Justice: God's Vision – Man's Discipleship* (Christmas pastoral letter; 1972).

9. *THE PRISONER AND THE CHURCHES*

1. Quoted by Gerald O'Collins, *Interpreting Jesus* (Geoffrey Chapman/Paulist Press, 1983), p. 74.
2. William Temple, *The Ethics of Punishment* (1930).
3. Carlo M. Martini, Cardinal Archbishop of Milan, at Domus Mariae, Rome (24 November 1983).
4. *Pastoral Constitution on the Church in the Modern World*, art. 27: *The Documents of Vatican II*, ed. W. M. Abbott, SJ (Geoffrey Chapman, 1966).
5. T. Morris, *Deviance and Control* (Hutchinson, 1976), p. 17.
6. *Report on the Work of the Prison Department 1974* (Cmnd 6148; HMSO), §193.

7. *Report on the Work of the Prison Department 1976* (Cmnd 6877; HMSO), §229.
8. *Report on the Work of the Prison Department 1977* (Cmnd 7290; HMSO), §200.
9. Reported in *The Tablet* (1 March 1986), p. 228.
10. *Message of the International Commission of Principal Prison Chaplains*, from the Congress held in Madrid, 9–13 September 1985.
11. *The Code of Canon Law* (English translation; Collins, 1983).
12. *The Reform of Correctional Institutions in the 1970's* (US Catholic Conference; November 1973).
13. *A Time for Justice* (Catholic Social Welfare Commission, 1982), §39.
14. Official report (24 March 1982), cols 988–989.
15. *Faith in the City* (Church House Publishing, 1985), chapter 14 *passim*.
16. *A Time for Justice, op. cit.*
17. *Punishment and Imprisonment* (Dominican Publications, 1985).
18. Adrian Speller, *Breaking Out* (Hodder and Stoughton, 1986).
19. *Ibid.*, p. 154.
20. *A Time for Justice, op. cit.*, §66.